GOD IS LOSER FRIENDLY

GOD IS LOSER FRIENDLY
Abraham, Isaac, Jacob, & Me

For Karen!

Tim W. Callaway

To ~~Dr. Dave~~ — with much admiration! Be graced! Again!

Jim

Vogelstein Press
Calgary, Alberta

God is Loser Friendly: Abraham, Isaac, Jacob, & Me

Copyright © 2020 by Tim W. Callaway

ISBN: 978–1–989977–02–6 (paperback)
ISBN: 978–1–989977–03–3 (epub)

Published by Vogelstein Press
Calgary, Alberta, Canada

Website: www.vogelsteinpress.com
Email: vogelsteinpress@shaw.ca

Cover artwork: Copyright © 2020 Elena MacKenzie Hiebert. Used by permission of the artist.
Cover layout & interior formatting: Trish Kotow

The views expressed in works published by Vogelstein Press are those of the author and do not necessarily represent the official position of Vogelstein Press.

All rights reserved. No part of this publication may be reproduced, stored in a retrieval system or transmitted, in any form, or by any means, electronic, mechanical, photocopying, scanning, recording, or otherwise without the author's prior permission. The only exception is for brief quotations used in reviews and articles.

Excerpt from *Saint & Sinners* by Lawrence Wright, copyright © 1993 by Lawrence Wright. Used by permission of Alfred A. Knopf, an imprint of the Knopf Doubleday Publishing Group, a division of Penguin Random House LLC. All rights reserved.

Excerpts from *Water to Wine* by Brian Zahnd, copyright © 2016 Spello Press and Brian Zahnd. Used by permission of the author.

Excerpts from *Genesis for Normal People* by Peter Enns and Jared Byas (2012 Patheos Press), copyright © Peter Enns and Jared Byas. Used by permission of the authors.

Excerpt from *The Power Worshippers: Inside the Dangerous Rise of Religious Nationalism* by Katherine Stewart, copyright © 2019 Katherine Stewart. Used by permission of Bloomsbury Publishing.

Excerpt(s) from *Plan B: Further Thoughts on Faith* by Anne Lamott, copyright © 2005 by Anne Lamott. Used by permission of Riverhead, an imprint of Penguin Publishing Group, a division of Penguin Random House LLC. All rights reserved.

Excerpt(s) from *Grace (Eventually): Thoughts on Faith* by Anne Lamott, copyright © 2007 by Anne Lamott. Used by permission of Riverhead, an imprint of Penguin Publishing Group, a division of Penguin Random House LLC. All rights reserved.

Excerpt(s) from *Stitches: A Handbook on Meaning, Hope and Repair* by Anne Lamott, copyright © 2013 by Anne Lamott. Used by permission of Riverhead, an imprint of Penguin Publishing Group, a division of Penguin Random House LLC. All rights reserved.

Excerpt(s) from *Genesis: A Living Conversation* by Bill Moyers, copyright © 1996 by Public Affairs Television. Used by permission of Doubleday, an imprint of the Knopf Doubleday Publishing Group, a division of Penguin Random House LLC. All rights reserved.

Excerpt(s) from *In the Beginning: A New Interpretation of Genesis* by Karen Armstrong, copyright © 1996 by Karen Armstrong. Used by permission of Alfred A. Knopf, an imprint of the Knopf Doubleday Publishing Group, a division of Penguin Random House LLC. All rights reserved.

Excerpts from Zondervan publications, including *The Purpose Driven Life* by Rick Warren, copyright © 2002 by Rick Warren; *What's So Amazing About Grace?* by Philip Yancey, copyright © 1997 by Philip D. Yancey; *Toward Old Testament Ethics* by Walter C. Kaiser, Jr., copyright © 1983 by The Zondervan Corporation; *Genesis: A Devotional Exposition* by Donald Grey Barnhouse, copyright © 1973 by Zondervan Publishing House; are used by permission of Zondervan www.zondervan.com.

Excerpt from *The Journals of Jim Elliot* by Elisabeth Elliot (ed.), copyright © 1978 by Elisabeth Elliot. Used by permission of Baker Publishing Group.

Excerpts from *Accidental Preacher*: A Memoir, by Will Willimon, copyright © 2019. Used by permission of Wm. B. Eerdmans Publishing Co.

Brief quotes from pp. 63-4, 65 of *Peculiar Treasures* by Frederick Buechner. Copyright © 1979 by Frederick Buechner. Illustration copyright (c) 1979 by Katherine A. Buechner. Used by permission of HarperCollins Publishers.

Brief quotes from pp. 172-3, 178 of *Secrets in the Dark* by Frederick Buechner. Copyright © 2006 by Frederick Buechner. Used by permission of HarperCollins Publishers.

Lyrics to *He'll Dry the Tears* in Chapter 10 used by permission of composer and artist, Dallas Holm.

for Joyce

"…Genesis has been treasured not for the light it throws on the irretrievably distant past but for its timeless relevance to the present … Our authors are not interested in historical accuracy, however. Instead they bring to the reader's attention important truths about the human predicament that still reverberate today."

>   Karen Armstrong,
>   *In the Beginning: A New Interpretation of Genesis*; 7.

"Genesis 12-50 is a story of Israel's ups and downs and how that roller coaster soap opera will pan out."

>   Peter Enns and Jared Byas,
>   *Genesis for Normal People*; x.

"You've got to love this in a God—consistently assembling the motleyest people to bring, into the lonely and frightening world, a commitment to caring and community. It's a centuries-long reality show—Moses the stutterer, Rahab the hooker, David the adulterer, Mary the homeless teenager. Not to mention all the mealy-mouthed disciples. Not to mention a raging insecure narcissist like me."

>   Anne Lamott,
>   *Plan B: Further Thoughts on Faith*; 22

"John Gardner tells us that history never looks like history when you are living through it. It looks confusing and messy, and always feels uncomfortable. You can certainly say that about history as we find it in the Book of Genesis. God is founding a dynasty, the beginnings of Judaism, Christianity, and Islam. One might expect the storyteller to paint the First Family ten feet tall with several coats of whitewash. But the picture we get of these men and women is uncomfortably human. There is so much marital conflict and sibling intrigue they almost forfeit the call and fumble the promise. Yet the storyteller refuses to clean up their act. This is the amazing thing about the people of Genesis. The more we talk about them, the more they look like people we know—faces in the mirror."

> Bill Moyers,
> *Genesis: A Living Conversation*; 155

"The God who chose Israel and the church is a sucker for the likes of me. You can look it up. Jesus begins his work not by a solo dive into ministry but by putting the finger on a dozen knuckleheads and commissioning them to do what he wants done in the world...."

> Will Willimon,
> *Accidental Preacher: A Memoir*; 55.

"It is exactly this bewildering, perverse and
paradoxical mixture of the saint
in the sinner and the sinner in the saint that I
find so compelling and revelatory
of the mysteriousness of the human
predicament."

Lawrence Wright, (1993)
Saints and Sinners, p. xvii

Table of Contents

Foreword	1
Introduction	3
Chapter One: We've Come a Long Way, Maybe	11
Chapter Two: Busload of GRACE to Get By	29
Chapter Three: My Name is Abraham, and I am a Liar (Genesis 12:1-13:4)	55
Chapter Four: When God Has the Last Laugh (Genesis 16-18, 21)	75
Chapter Five: The Mess at Sodom (Genesis 18-19)	93
Chapter Six: Laughter; Or Not (Genesis 26:1-28:9)	107
Chapter Seven: She's Good With Camels, Not So Good With Children (Genesis 25-27)	117
Chapter Eight: Just Call Me "Jake, the Snake" (Genesis 27-35)	133
Chapter Nine: Out Come the Claws (Genesis 29-35)	151

Chapter Ten: Skeletons in the Family Closet (Genesis 38)	161
Chapter Eleven: Celebrating a Reckless Grace	175
Epilogue	181
Acknowledgements	185
Bibliography	187
For Further Reading	195
Index	197

Foreword

There are very few theological writers who can get my attention through humour and then walk over and look at the "loser" in the mirror and thank the grace of God. Tim Callaway has been consistently doing this for me for several years, first as his youth and CE pastor, and then over numerous cups of coffee in a galaxy close to home, first in Calgary and then Edmonton, Tim taught me a great aphorism to guide a young pastor, to "beware of the libel of labels" which I was prone to gravitate towards in my early theological naivete. He demonstrated this truism in practice through a series of sermons that he titled "God is Loser Friendly." They came at a time when we were raising a toddler daughter, and then a second, and finally a third (who are now in their twenties) and we were as disheveled and scattered as new parents could be and needed words that would show desperately needed, as one author says: "cracks of grace." At an all time low in our perceived competency, we heard illustrated what I had been learning with words like "covenant," but in a way that guided my reading of the Old Testament in a manner which lofty theological tomes could not adequately express.

As Tim states here: "contrary to what many of us may have been led to believe, the Old Testament is not solely preoccupied with The Law or The Torah. But let there be no obscurity about it: the Old Testament prominently evidences the grace of God right from its opening pages ... Grace is found or received, not won." Then he comes right out and tells it like it is: "To repeat, then, I call such people "losers," not to be disrespectful or dismissive of them, but because, like you and me, they were often their own worst enemies when it came to pursuing a life that might be considered remotely worthy of the grace granted them."

Those sermons which have been reworked and revised for this book helped me step off the treadmill of working harder and harder to make Jesus love me and, through the stories of losers in the Old Testament, allowed me to rest in a way to know I am loved by a God much bigger than we can imagine.

Tim's words are our invitation: "So laugh along with me not so much to excuse yourself as to celebrate the amazing and amusing grace of the God who, for his own purposes alone, chose to reach out and put his hand on your shoulder as an expression of his desire to be in relationship with you. As you read, I hope you will encounter an even greater amazement at God's inexplicable kindness not only in initially gracing you, but in continuing to grace you despite the numerous reminders all of us regularly encounter regarding how far we have yet to go in terms of getting it all together."

Tim has never asked me, nor does he ask us in this book, to always agree with him or treat him like a guru because he has the gift of comforting the afflicted and afflicting the comfortable. Rather, he will challenge you to hear what Steve Brown calls "the beautiful laughter of the Redeemed," or as Tim would say, "the laughter of redeemed losers."

So, prepare to wrestle, laugh and be challenged by this remarkable journey of loser-soaked grace.

Bryan Clarke, PhD
Instructor; Reformed Presbyterian Chaplain
University of Alberta, Edmonton

Introduction

American mega-church pastor Rick Warren appropriately identified a foundational component of divine grace when he opened his best-selling book, *The Purpose Driven Life* (2002), with this bold declaration: "It's not about you!" (p. 17)

Millions of people considered his insight to have evident relevance for our mothers-in-law and brothers-in-law. We therefore purchased Warren's work in substantial quantities for various pain-in-the-neck relatives, cranky neighbours, exasperating co-workers and fellow-churchgoers, hopeful they would all read at least the first paragraph. Thus it was that the book became one of the best-selling volumes in the history of North American religious publishing.

Most of us are comfortable with the popular adage "it's not about you" as excellent advice. For somebody else. For those who regularly attend worship services, it is similar to our conviction that the guilt-inducing sermon we heard not long ago by our pastor is precisely what Henry next door needs to hear. The same goes for Gina in our book club. If only they would haul their derrieres out of bed and get to church sometime before they render their final exhalation.

Should we be truly honest, however—the kind of candour that periodically creeps up and startles us while standing alone in our walk-in closets—we ought to willingly, if reluctantly, admit we are among the billions that pursue life as if it actually *is* all about us.

That being so, should God in this digital era be utilizing emoticons in his or her data-entry system, the first notation in whatever kind of files s/he is keeping on me likely looks exactly like the now-famous eye-roll emoji. At least two or three such images would be necessarily affixed to the records of each of my siblings.

In no way is my opening indictment intended to suggest that believers ought to spiritually flagellate ourselves for our ample inventory of inconsistencies. Rather, as this book attempts to illuminate, there are actually many reasons to be encouraged in our walk of faith while simultaneously recognizing there is room for improvement in the daunting pursuit of being a credible disciple of Jesus Christ.

I say this because, as I aim to demonstrate in this work, "it's all about me" has long been the norm in the thinking and behaviour of some very devout people. In fact, a popular ancient record, The Holy Bible, documents that humankind has relentlessly prioritized self-interest from the earliest of times.

This accurate—if bothersome—reality is in primary focus throughout this series of essays. The Old Testament record of Genesis reveals that many, perhaps most, of our spiritual forebears shamelessly lived as if it was indeed "all about me."

That's right, many of God's favourite people were also masters at selfishly breaking one or more of the Ten Commandments on any given day. They worshipped other gods and sometimes fashioned graven images; they dishonoured their fathers and mothers; some committed murder and adultery while others stole, bore false witness and coveted their neighbour's stuff.

You are already feeling better about yourself, are you not? So am I.

A word of caution may be in order at the outset of this investigation. For various reasons, some readers may be uncomfortable with how I have turned the twenty-first century spotlight on these early figures in the Old Testament narrative. You may be troubled by the absence of a lengthy disclaimer acknowledging my awareness of the dissimilarity in culture or the manner of how humans related to God that prevailed in an ancient era.

Thanks for raising the point. For better or worse, such is a conscious choice I have made in an effort to promote our identification with these Biblical characters. Contrary to what you may have been taught or assume and believe, they were everyday guys and gals who were prone to all of the human frailties that we possess. Hopefully, it will become apparent as you read that I am indeed mindful of some of the significant differences between the realities of an ancient era and our own concerning how people engage and are engaged by the Almighty.

It should also be recognized, of course, that to critique our ancestors in the faith too harshly or to lament them as unique in their failings would be unfair, unkind and inaccurate. *Au contraire*, it would be equally unfair, unkind and inaccurate to deify them to the point of altogether missing the valuable insights to be gleaned from a candid assessment of their lives. After all, the original writer(s) of Genesis was/were exceptionally frank in detailing the shortcomings of the ancients.

Perfect people, like you and me, they certainly were not. What they were was perfectly human.

This book assumes a truth so obvious that it is humbling if not embarrassing to recognize how consistently it has been overlooked by many readers of Scripture. That is: there is a definite sense in which the Holy Bible is a record of a broad assortment of spiritual "losers." The Old Testament icons examined here were head of the class when it came to demonstrating how to blunder, botch and bungle the golden opportunities they encountered for modeling even a modest degree of spiritual maturity.

Perhaps I should also clarify that by using the term "loser," I do not intend to offend or to support any version of psycho-theology that suggests there is nothing innately redemptive about humanity. I readily affirm that the *imago Dei* is resident in all people and am not interested in contributing to any so-called "worm theology" by my use of the term "loser." By employing this designation, I have in mind what any standard dictionary defines as "a person who seems destined to fail repeatedly." Trust me, I unreservedly include myself in this population.

In any event, we are wise to refrain from being too disapproving of the more than adequate job both the older and younger modern generations of believers today are doing as it relates to emulating the ancients with our persistent self-centred approaches to life. God, it seems, has always maintained a passionate affinity for offering his unfailing friendship and goodness to the Homer Simpsons of any given period of history.

Given the self-absorbed worldview so prominently featured in modern North American culture, some of us might hasten to defend our affinity for thinking "it's all about me" as being somewhat excusable if not altogether inevitable. "You'd better believe I'm unashamedly looking out for *numero uno*," we might object. "That's because, COVID-19 notwithstanding, it is a fair generality to conclude that nobody else is!"

It is small surprise, then, that this is the attitude we implicitly communicate by how we live. We recognize, of course, that modern consumers are bombarded 24/7 with the subtle insinuation: "Psst, it *is indeed* all about you! NO, REALLY! IT *IS* ALL ABOUT *YOU*!" Such a message and its accompanying worldview are spewed at us, for example, via the endless parade of creative and alluring communication devices that dominate everyday life.

Since Rick Warren first penned the arresting assertion referred to above, the imaginative capabilities of entrepreneurial minds have been tirelessly at work. Behind the ubiquitous e-devices that have more power over our lives than we even recognize is a sly manner of thinking that conditions us to be even more adept at ignoring Warren's caution.

Contemporary capitalist society offers no shortage of urgent promotions for that next electronics upgrade that we must absolutely and immediately acquire. That particular device then becomes but one more item on an endless menu of essential products that, via the employment of some prize-winning spiritual gymnastics, we eventually convince ourselves is a true necessity rather than a mere luxury. That we have yet to come anywhere close to mastering the astounding capabilities of the current version of a similar gizmo we already possess is largely irrelevant to persuading ourselves we need to be at the front of the line the day iPhone XV hits the stores.

We owe it to ourselves, or so we are brazenly counselled by the wise guys in Silicon Valley, to immediately obtain the latest and greatest combination of these comparatively tiny instruments of plastic and titanium. As Naomi Klein has capably documented, the advertising sector has long since laid claim to any available space encountered within one's field of vision during a typical day. These compelling messages are therefore virtually impossible to overlook or ignore (Klein, 2000, pp. 35–45).

And so, we cave. We observe, listen, calculate and, before we know it, are rushing out to the nearest Apple outlet to UPgrade, thereby succumbing to a pressure that—buyer beware—may very well also serve to simultaneously DEgrade our earnest desires and efforts to live a less self-oriented life. In so doing, we authenticate a pattern of thinking that is deserving of ongoing careful scrutiny by anyone at all desirous of living in light of the teachings of Jesus or of Scripture's directive to not permit popular society to squeeze us into its mold (Romans 12:1, 2).

This is not to say that we do not incur pangs of guilt on occasion for capitulating to such a mindset. Or that we do not feverishly determine to be more diligent next time in our efforts to withstand audacious marketing schemes. So, I hasten to emphasize that my indictment regarding our succumbing to society's pressures is not intended to needlessly shame or guilt readers.

Rather, the primary objective in the pages ahead is to offer insight and inspiration for thoughtful reflection to those who consider another best-selling book, the Bible, to be an admirable authority that has much yet to teach us about navigating the roiling waves on the seas of contemporary life.

In contemplating some of the behavioural templates the Biblical record unveils in its opening narrative, Genesis, it is quickly evident that our inclination to a stubborn preoccupation with that which affects us personally is reasonable. We are simply doing what has always been done by our predecessors, that which seems to have come very naturally even to people of great faith. In other words, self-serve has been around since long before the service station down the street standardized it a few decades ago.

It is one of my primary goals here to motivate readers of some amount of Christian faith—or no amount of Christian faith—to engage in critical thinking concerning how easy it can be to embrace the subtle presuppositions of a culture that is driven, controlled and measured by unfettered economic capitalism. If you are anything like me, it is often not until after I have faltered yet again into conformity with popular thinking in this regard that I even realize the identity of the formidable creature that came knocking at my door.

What I have written here, therefore, is designed to confront, correct and challenge my own thinking as much as the thinking of anyone else.

****

> "As Americans we are given a script from birth—it is our shared and assumed formula for the pursuit of happiness. Without even being aware of it we are scripted in the belief that our superior technology, our self-help ideology, our dominant military, and our capacity to obtain consumer goods should guarantee our happiness—our ticket to Paradise. Said just so, it sounds silly, but when it is communicated in the liturgies of advertising and the propaganda of state, it becomes believable ... and we do believe it. **Give me a new iPhone, a motivational talk, a trillion-dollar war machine, a Visa card, and I can be happy!** For the most part the Americanized church has unconsciously bought into this script and concocted a compromised

Christianity to endorse the script point for point. It's Americanism with a Jesus fish bumper sticker … The Enlightenment promise that technology would lead to Utopia has been weighed in the balances of history and found wanting. It went up in smoke— **literal smoke!**—in the gray ashes of Auschwitz and a hideous mushroom cloud over Hiroshima. Gullible faith in the ability of technology to automatically produce a better world should now be seen as a naïve anachronism." (Zahnd, 2016, pp. 26–27) (emphasis original)

Chapter One:
We've Come a Long Way, Maybe

The problem with God—or at any rate, one of the top five most annoying things about God—is that He or She rarely answers right away. It can take days, weeks. Some people seem to understand this—that life and change take time. Chou En-lai, when asked, "What do you think of the French Revolution?" paused for a minute—smoking incessantly—then replied, "Too soon to tell."
(Anne Lamott, 2005, p. 9)

Some of you reading these words likely grew up during the 1960s as I did within the tightly controlled world of North American fundagelical Christianity. (I credit my younger brother and popular evangelical author, Phil Callaway, for coining the term "fundagelical" years ago in a magazine article where I first encountered it. His story titled *Up in Smoke* was later published in one of his books (2002, p. 60). Although I subsequently wrote a doctoral dissertation in religious history wherein I attempted to articulate the difference(s) between fundamentalism and evangelicalism, I have never encountered Phil's term in wide use in academia. I have nonetheless frequently employed it in my academic involvements because its etymology accurately describes the historic connection that indeed exists between American religious fundamentalism and modern North American evangelicalism. Where you have one, you will invariably have at least some attributes of the other (Tim W. Callaway, 2013, pp. 40–90)).

As anyone raised in such an environment remembers, attendance at worship services (morning AND evening), Sunday school, youth group, family devotions, Backyard Bible Club, Daily Vacation Bible School and Bible memorization initiatives, *et cetera*, were staples of that particular subculture. My siblings and I participated in them all.

I am grateful for many of those early experiences, if for no other reason than that I possess a vast supply of hilarious accounts that I can and do relate concerning youthful antics carried out (for research purposes!) while active in such. I was fortunate enough to be born into a home where humour and laughter were basic ingredients of our existential diet, thereby assisting us in the challenge of surviving the ever-present strictures of rigid fundamentalism.

As the years passed, however, I came to recognize that a dark cloud loitered behind some of those silver linings. In hindsight, I realize that such traditions may actually have contributed to the acquisition of a more sanctified version of the "it's all about me" mindset that is in the crosshairs of my thinking in this volume.

For example, we were taught from infancy to revere the godly characters of the Bible such as Abraham, Isaac, Jacob, Moses, Miriam, Esther, Ruth, David, and Jezebel.

Okay, Jezebel? Not so much. Via such avenues as lengthy sermons and weekly Christian education hours augmented by a healthy roster of Christian films and books, we were routinely exhorted as youngsters to pattern ourselves after Biblical luminaries and urged to emulate their examples of admirable faith. Although the spiritual failings of these characters may not have been entirely overlooked, they were certainly minimized in favour of focusing on the godlier attributes of the respective personalities.

Additionally, those of us who populated the fundagelical ethos that flourished in the second half of the twentieth century were prompted to follow in the footsteps of virtuous Christian heroes of more recent eras. By means of local church missionary conferences and "biography nights," related films, filmstrips and slide shows, we were exposed to inspiring accounts of missionary icons such as David Livingstone, Gladys Aylward, J. Hudson Taylor, Isobel

Kuhn, Borden of Yale, Amy Carmichael, Jim and Elizabeth Elliot, and others of lesser renown.

I have frequently explained to those who inquire as to why I trained to become a pastor that it is essential they understand the ideological milieu in which I was raised. The ultimate vocation held out to us as impressionable children was to become a foreign missionary in some far-off region of the world. There, ideally, we would be eaten by cannibals since in the words of Jesus in Acts 1:8, "you shall be my witnesses," the Greek word for "witnesses" is "marturioi" from which the English term "martyrs" derives. Should we have failed to achieve this Grade A, Canada #1 level of Christian commitment, only then was it permissible to settle for the solitary other acceptable vocational pursuit—becoming a pastor or otherwise engaging in some variety of home-missions work. (I do not relate this to be unnecessarily critical or cynical; such an ethos was truly the consciously created reality of the faith community in which I was raised. Many peers from those days have confirmed my assessment in this regard as accurate).

In the fundamentalist home where I grew up, a proper observance of Sundays required us to put aside our *Hardy Boys* mysteries and *Chip Hilton* sports thrillers in honour of reading material considered more suitable for "The Lord's Day" as Sundays were usually called in those days. In lieu of such comparatively mundane literature, we were directed to volumes from Christian publishers such as Moody Press and Zondervan extolling loftier values like those found in the *Danny Orlis*, *Felicia Cartwright*, *Sugar Creek Gang* series of books and other similar tales. (Interestingly enough, I have since encountered a very insightful unpublished doctoral thesis on the fundamentalist self as such was portrayed in the *Danny Orlis* books (Peters, 1996)).

My parents ensured that missionary biographies were numerous on our bookshelves and frequently invited visiting missionaries into our home for lodging or a meal. Accordingly, by the time I reached my teenage years, I was certain I had experienced more divine calls to various mission fields than Heinz has pickles.

Early in life, then, I became conversant with the fascinating and often miraculous details of the lives of the heroes of the Bible and other figures in subsequent Christian history. Our parents, teachers and other spiritual leaders challenged and even bribed us to memorize entire chapters of Scripture. It was their fervent hope that we would grasp and adapt the attitudes and behaviours that made these figures such exemplary models of faith.

When I was in elementary school, for example, my parents once promised to reward me with a genuine leather football for reading through the Pentateuch—in the original Hebrew, no less. Not really. I accomplished the challenge in the King James Version which was only minimally easier and thereby earned the football. (My theologically trained friends insist that the trauma I incurred at such an impressionable age is the only reason I adhere today to the post-tribulation stance in my eschatology. In fact, they are adamant in their collective conviction that I survived The Great Tribulation several times during my upbringing).

As children in Sunday School we sang songs like *Only a Boy Named David*, *Dare to Be a Daniel* or *I Will Make You Fishers of Men* as part of a carefully crafted regimen designed to help us acquire and demonstrate the enviable virtues modeled by ancient Bible characters. *How Did Moses Cross the Red Sea?* was one of my childhood favourites if for no other reason than that a fellow scallywag would usually be compensated with a stern rebuke from the teacher(s) for adding some very creative choreography to what, in those days, were called "action choruses."

Many of us—entire families in some cases—were given first names in accordance with what were identified back in the day as "Bible names." For instance, I knew early in life that my parents had named me for the Apostle Paul's spiritual protégé, Timothy, a name composed from two Greek words combined to mean "one who honours God" or "honouring God." They harboured fervent hopes that each of their five children would grow up to be people of sterling Christian character. My siblings were named David, Daniel, Ruth, Philip and Tiffany.

Sorry, no Tiffany, although my sister's orthodoxy did come under scrutiny a few years back when she decreed that, henceforth, she wished to be called Carolyn, (her actual first name) and not Ruth (her actual second name) as she had previously been known. Disciplinary hearings are in progress.

Given the environment of my formative years, it strikes me now that we came to view the legendary characters of the Bible as a variation of sorts of what our community regarded to be the errant Roman Catholic Church's beliefs regarding saints. True, we were not encouraged to ask these Biblical icons for some kind of mysterious assistance. Yet we were certainly expected to look up to them as being far superior to us in matters of faith and conduct. And we were also directed to spare no effort in striving to emulate them since they were almost always presented to us as unfailing in their devotion and purity.

Looking back, I see that such personalities always seemed somewhat removed from the reality of our lives by virtue of what we as children perceived to be a kind of super-spirituality. We concluded that, surely, these Biblical figures never told off colour jokes, used "swear words" or smoked cigarettes behind the local drugstore. They had made it into the Bible, hadn't they? How much of the Torah did they have to memorize to get such a gig? Many were listed in Hebrews 11 that was commonly represented to those of us who were sports enthusiasts as "The Hall of Faith."

Few of us in those halcyon days retained much hope of ever rivalling the main characters found in the Bible in terms of the maturity of their exemplary faith. We were content to simply give it our best shot and gladly absorb the periodic compliments our parents and leaders would periodically send our way for demonstrating, in some small way, the faith of a Joseph, a Joshua, an Isaiah or an Elizabeth.

It was not until later in life that I began to see the well-intentioned but nevertheless myopic perspective that made us view the characters of the Bible as some kind of spiritual supermen or superwomen. What surprised me not a little when that revelation occurred was the fact that the Bible very clearly indicates that most personalities in Genesis did not live up to such noble designations.

Not at all.

Was blind but now I see

I had been a pastor in the evangelical sector for about ten years before a warming theological discovery registered with me during a frosty Canadian winter. For reasons I will shortly clarify, I read through the first book of the Bible, Genesis, only to have it become apparent to me as never before that, in fact, some of the heroes of the faith I had come to revere while a child definitely were not the spiritual giants I had assumed them to be. John S. Kselman hits the nail squarely on the head in this respect by asking: "What do you make of the fact that every family in Genesis is a fractured family—what we would call a "dysfunctional" family?" (Moyers, (ed.), 1996, pp. 26–28).

In other words, despite the pristine personalities that had been bestowed on these figures by well-meaning adults during my upbringing, I realized that most of the prominent figures in Genesis are actually portrayed as having had major character flaws. They were indeed far from the noble examples of faith I had heard about in my childhood and that I had somehow continued to envision even through numerous years of religious and theological training.

When read at face value, the Genesis record could not be clearer that most of those I had grown up hearing referred to as heroes of the faith were, in fact, people who truly knew how to really screw things up. For the first time in my life, I began to comprehend that fellows like Abraham, Isaac and Jacob could well have spent their fair share of time in the principal's office for behaviour unbecoming. I saw, with no small satisfaction, that they could easily have received as many detentions in high school as I had earned. These guys were self-seekers, par excellent. They each had an ample personal inventory of rough edges and serious shortcomings in their lives.

Character flaws? Stumbling blocks? Progress yet to be made in their spiritual development? For sure, the evidence is abundant! And it is right there in plain view in the pages of Genesis for their spiritual posterity to review in all of its arresting candour and brazen faithlessness.

How had I missed such even as an adult—a theologically trained adult at that?

It registered with me that winter as never before that when you read these stories for what the text actually reveals without allowing anyone else to contextualize them for you, many of the revered figures in Genesis are not very nice people at all. Frankly, I am not certain I would have been comfortable living next door to some of them. Nor would I have considered leaving my kids in their care or getting involved in a business transaction with people of their ilk.

Karen Armstrong augments the point very well when she writes:

> "In this story of God's chosen family, we find very few of the "family values" that Jews, Christians, and Muslims, who all in their different ways claim to be children of Abraham, avow as crucial to the religious life. Abraham's household was a troubled one; in no way did it replicate the lost harmony of Eden." (Armstrong, 1996, pp. 64–65)

Two incidents from my everyday world came together that winter to open my spiritual eyes to these Bible heroes as I had never before considered them. Such myopia was largely owing to the fact that, as I have indicated, my childhood and much of my vocational training occurred within the fundagelical orbit. As honest students of any particular interpretation of Christianity (insert the appropriate adjective for your brand) should acknowledge, all traditional interpretations of the Christian faith come with their fair share of cultural, historical, exegetical, hermeneutical and denominational baggage.

It was in the mid-1990s, then, that I read about a series of upcoming Public Broadcasting System television programs to be hosted by respected American journalist, Bill Moyers. Since I was familiar with and appreciative of Moyers' work, I made plans to record the conversations that were proposed featuring a panel of academic and religious experts as they related to the curious realities conveyed in the narratives found in Genesis. I read the relevant passages from Genesis beforehand that were scheduled to be discussed in each weekly program. I later acquired the book *Genesis: A Living Conversation* (a companion to the public television series) edited by Moyers and published thereafter that contained the transcripts of those interactions (Moyers, (Ed.), 1996).

Bill Moyers and his diverse roster of well qualified guests capably documented that the first book of the Bible graphically informs us that most of the key figures in the early pages of the book revered by Christians were people with major—indeed, jaw-dropping—character flaws. They were consistently self-seeking, dishonest, cunning, dysfunctional, vengeful, immoral, and untrustworthy, to name but a few of their individual and collective fortes. Many of them were more qualified for what some people today might call a "shyster" than for inclusion among God's chosen people. (I make no apology whatsoever and, and am indeed delighted to report especially for the benefit of my legal and political friends, that an old online *Encarta* dictionary I consulted for a fine tuning of the term "shyster" states: "an unscrupulous person, especially a lawyer and a political representative." Nailed it! So, to those of my acquaintances for whom such a designation is relevant, would you please deal with the matter in question? Thank you!).

Contrary to the messages many of us absorbed as children about the ancient figures of the Bible being iconic examples of great faith, then, there are glaring elements in their lives that indicate they were not "winners" at all. They were better qualified as "losers," those well deserving of being on the receiving end of the modern expressions by which we often communicate perplexity: "Really!?" "Seriously!?" or "Are you kidding me!?"

Any parent who has ever been tempted to give up on their own child(ren) achieving a commendable level of spiritual maturity ought to derive significant comfort and encouragement from what the book of Genesis reveals concerning God's experiences in coping with the antics of some of his "kids." Here we find them, portrayed for billions of readers over the numerous centuries to encounter, sitting atop their pile of dirty laundry directly in front of the skeletons in their closets.

The honour roll

At around the same time I was tuning in to Bill Moyers and his team's intriguing discussions on PBS, the current issue of *Maclean's*, Canada's weekly newsmagazine, arrived in the mail. *Maclean's* was published for decades in Canada and covered the nation's political and cultural life. In 2016, like many other print media publications in the internet era, it changed its primary identity to an online publication although it continues to publish a monthly paper edition.

Maclean's at that time would publish an Honour Roll every January in which it identified a number of Canadians who had figured prominently in the nation's news the previous calendar year. In addition to some of the predictable personalities that all such lists contain—sports figures, entertainers, politicians—profile was also given to a number of rank and file Canadians considered to have made particularly positive contributions to their communities during the preceding year.

As I read through the *Maclean's* cover story one evening prior to tuning in the Moyers TV series, I found myself wondering if anyone had ever considered publishing—not an Honour Roll of

Winners, but an Honour Roll of Losers. Or, instead of an Honour Roll, a Dishonour Roll. You know, formally publicize a list of citizens who had really botched it during the past year—Canadians who had resoundingly messed up—so the entire nation could read and recall.

Now, apart from the fact that I come from a healthy lineage of jokers, why would I ponder the merits of publishing an Honour Roll for Losers?

Short answer: blame the Bible or Genesis. Do not fault Bill Moyers or his contingent of competent scholars. They did not write the material they were analyzing. Regardless of your view of matters related to the inspiration and authority of Scripture—maybe blame the Holy Spirit or Moses. Perhaps blame JEPD. (JEPD is the abbreviation for a component of critical scholarship that posits the first five books of The Old Testament as the work of several writers/editors as opposed to the traditional view of fundagelicals that Genesis represents the work of a single author, likely Moses).

I really do not care what decision you make in this regard except to say that if you are inclined to view the Bible as any kind of a reliable guide for how to live in the modern era, recognize your obligation to come to terms with the tabloid quality news stories dispensed in the opening chapters of what is often referred to as "The Good Book."

Because I again submit to you that for many of us—perhaps for most of us—such sordid details as we find in Genesis might best be received as a unique kind of comfort and affirmation. They should enter our field of spiritual vision as good news and as welcome relief. We are not alone in our persistent spiritual dysfunctions! In fact, we are in fairly reputable company with respect to succumbing to spiritual breakdown.

"Hallelujah," I can hear some of you saying. "You mean to tell me that I am not the first ridiculously inconsistent joker that God has had to put up with?" Or "are you suggesting there are people in the Bible who believed one thing and lived another, people whose behaviour did not live up to their theology?"

Yes, I am indeed positing precisely that scenario.

An anecdote from a recent newspaper story regarding congregational life at one church in British Columbia underscores the point I wish to make here. One Sunday morning, Pastor Jeff Germo invited parishioners to take out their smartphones during a worship service and interact with him electronically via a communications technology developed in Sweden:

> At the church auditorium in Campbell River, Mr. Germo started his sermon by asking parishioners to take out their smartphones and tablets, click on a Mentimeter link and punch in a code.
>
> Moments later, an e-mail arrived asking parishioners if they have ever failed terribly.
>
> Just 2 per cent replied: "No, I'm a winner."
>
> Mr. Germo expressed amazement that any member of the congregation said they had never experienced failure.
>
> "If you are more than a year old, you probably have failed at something," Mr. Germo said as a man at the back of the auditorium of about 250 people raised his hand to acknowledge he chose the 'no failure' answer.
>
> "That's beautiful. That's delusional," Mr. Germo jokes.
>
> But as the sermon continued, large display screens showed the majority of the survey participants replied they have experienced failure and are trying to get over it. (Meisnner, 2018)

Indeed! This excerpt is precisely in line with the reality of what is seen when we read the Biblical text for what it clearly states. To see ourselves in the failures of those heroes of faith whom God used, blessed and graced despite their penchant to seriously mess up, is essential to acquiring the hope that arises from a meaningful grasp of the essence of divine grace.

This, then, is what I have in mind when I talk in terms of truly comprehending that pursuing a life of faith is really not about me or us. It is actually about Something and Someone far more significant than either you or me.

And, for this fact, we ought to individually and collectively offer deep gratitude.

Welcome to the 21st century

The insights into the less than stellar behaviours of the characters of Genesis that the Moyers panel and book presented combined with my musings regarding the *Maclean's* honour roll were augmented by yet another engaging influence I encountered along this line shortly into the twenty-first century. That was when I first read *Genesis for Normal People: A Guide to the Most Controversial, Misunderstood, and Abused Book of the Bible* co-authored by Peter Enns and Jared Byas and published in 2012. Their suggestions regarding the authorship and the time when the writing of The Pentateuch was finalized resonated with my own efforts to fit the stories to be visited in this book into the broader narrative of the Old Testament as a whole.

I am accordingly grateful for their insightful scholarship as evidenced by my use of a few lengthy quotations from their work:

> ...[T]he Pentateuch *as we know it* didn't come together until sometime after 539 B.C. (about 700–1000 years after the period of Moses). This is a significant year for Jews. The year 539 B.C. is when the Persian King Cyrus defeated the Babylonians, thus releasing the Israelites who had been captives of Babylon since 586 B.C.

> When we say the Pentateuch "as we know it" came together sometime after 539 B.C., we do not mean to say it was written from scratch during that time. There were certainly older writings and oral traditions that had been around for hundreds of years. But it was sometime after the Israelites returned to their homeland that all of these older writings and oral traditions were compiled and edited in the way we now have them in our Bible. So rather than viewing the Pentateuch as a song written by one artist at one time, it should be seen as a remix that takes samples of other work and puts them together in a fresh way to tell a single story. This goes for Genesis too.
>
> Why would anyone come to this conclusion? Because there are clues in Genesis that point you in this direction, some of which have been noted by Jewish and Christian readers for hundreds of years.
>
> For example, in the Abraham story (Genesis 12:6 and 13:7) we read that the Canaanites were living in the land "then" or "at that time." If the Canaanites were living in the land "then," it makes sense that the writer is writing at a time when the Canaanites were *not* in the land. And according to the biblical story, it wasn't until the days of Kings David and Solomon that the Canaanites were driven out, which was sometime after 1000 B.C. So here we have a clue that at least that part of Genesis comes from sometime after 1000 B.C., although it is telling us a story set in Abraham's day (about 2100 B.C., as the Bible presents it). (pp. 7–8) (emphasis original)

Against this informative background, Enns and Byas continue:

> Writing Israel's story probably started around the time of King David, but it went into hyperspeed when the Israelites went through the trauma of the exile as they were taken out of their country and into Babylon in the sixth century B.C. Why would that make them write more? The Israelites believed God

had promised, ages earlier, to give them the land of Canaan to be theirs forever. He also promised that they would have a line of kings descended from King David who would reign from Jerusalem forever. (You can read about this in 2 Samuel 7.) But Israel (especially the kings) had blown God off for so long that, as the story goes, God gave them over to their enemies, the Babylonians—who had recently become the superpower.

The Babylonians marched into Jerusalem and by 586 B.C. had bulldozed the Temple, God's sacred house, and taken much of the population captive. So in 586 B.C. Israel looked around. No king. No land. No Temple. Who is Israel without a king, without a land, and without the Temple? It looked like God had broken his promise and abandoned his own people.

It's not hard to imagine, then, why the Israelites at this time did some soul searching. They looked back at their ancient past to make sense of the tragedy of their recent history. "In view of all that happened, are we still God's people? Does he still care for us? How can we make sure that this doesn't happen to us again? Will we ever regain the glory of our past? To address these very real and pressing questions, they began retelling their story—one last time. That last telling became what Christians call the Old Testament.

> Think of the Old Testament as Israel's story, written in light of national trauma, to encourage continued faithfulness to God.

... The Pentateuch is Israel's constitution. "This is who we are, this is where we have come from, this is what we believe—and most importantly, this is what our God is like. He has always been faithful to us in the past, no matter how badly we screwed up. But he also commands us to be faithful. Let's make

> sure we remember all of this so we aren't carried off by another nation ever again."
>
> ... We have spent this chapter saying something rather simple: you cannot properly understand Genesis without seeing it first in *its* context, not ours. Genesis not only begins the story of Israel and should be read in conversation with the rest of that story, but it is also a story that is told through the eyes of an ancient people in national crisis." (pp. 8–11) (emphasis original)

As Enns and Byas helpfully confirm, much of the Old Testament amounts to a story of Israel's struggle with God and with becoming the people of God that he desired them to become. It is most fitting, therefore, that the book of Genesis contains several accounts regarding how desperately even the founding fathers (and mothers) of the people of God struggled in terms of their own faith. Stated succinctly, they come across to modern readers of Genesis as bumbling losers whose faith was not very exemplary at all. To cite Enns and Byas in this regard:

> If you need more convincing that struggling is a big issue in Genesis, look at Jacob. He literally wrestles with God and his new name, "Israel," means "one who struggles with God." This is exactly what we would expect from a story written by exiled Israelites who are struggling with their current conditions, and ultimately, their very identity." (p. 17)

Seeing the good news in bad news

Having been a pastor for more than three decades, I have encountered hundreds of people who have long since wearied of being consistently obstructed and ultimately defeated in their faith journey by their annoying personal character flaws, bad habits and conscious sins. They have often come to visit me when they are spiritually exhausted by persistent character weaknesses that have sabotaged their self respect, their earnest efforts and their spiritual vitality.

They tell me that their attempts to practice some kind of a meaningful life of faith have become useless to the point where they believe they are merely going through the motion of devotion. They are doing the best they can to maintain a semblance of orthodox faith in order to please their spouse and Christian friends (or their pastor), to set a good example for their kids or to preserve a carefully groomed reputation of being somewhat devout. Deep down, however, they are convinced that those "besetting sins," to reference the King James Version in Hebrews 12:1, have prompted God to give up on their ever being of any use to his Church or to his sovereign purposes.

If you can especially relate to such sentiments, trust me when I suggest that your experience is not as unusual as you may think it is or have been led to believe it is. Pursuing a life of faith in the twenty-first century requires painstaking, sustained and disciplined effort. It demands a tenacity that is fraught with frequent failure. It involves starting over again, time after time.

I know this because the Bible tells me so. So does my own experience together with that of scores of delightful men and women who over the years have been honest enough to confide in me their frustrations along this line.

I therefore cannot declare it strongly enough throughout this volume, for it needs to be trumpeted as revitalizing and regenerating news to all of us: GOD IS LOSER FRIENDLY! Or, to put it another way and thereby reconnect with Rick Warren's assertion: "It's not about you!"

For far too long now, too many of us for reasons related to our upbringing or otherwise, have engaged the life of faith as if it really is all about us. We have grown used to struggling along as best we can in our earnest efforts to attain our noblest objectives. Such an approach to the life of God-awareness is built on a false notion coloured by the inevitable influences of the culture in which we function. The essence of grace is otherwise for, as we will see, it is both counter-cultural and counter-intuitive.

That grace is "not of yourselves, so that no one can boast" is not a notion that began or made its debut with St. Paul in Ephesians 2:8, 9. It's a truth that God sets forth time and time again in the opening chapters of the first book in the Bible, Genesis. It may help you to think of it this way: grace tenaciously declared its arrival at the very beginning of time and is instructively recorded from the very outset of the Christian Scriptures.

Grace, then, is all about him or her, whatever pronoun for the Almighty best resonates with you. Yes, God has been rolling his or her eyes over the behaviour of well-intentioned people like you and me for millennia now. As you will see repeatedly throughout this work, I keep having this mental image of the Deity clapping himself or herself on the forehead and doing their best "Doh!" impression concerning the behaviour of their alleged loyalists. In truth, such has been the case since long before that esteemed professor of practical theology, Homer Simpson, ever introduced that term into contemporary conversation.

Chapter Two:
Busload of GRACE to Get By

You can't depend on any churches,
unless there's real estate you want to buy
You can't depend on a lot of things,
you need a busload of faith to get by
Busload of faith to get by, busload of faith to get by
Busload of faith to get by, busload of faith to get by

You can't depend on no miracle, you can't depend on the air
You can't depend on a wise man,
you can't find 'em because they're not there
Busload of faith to get by, busload of faith to get by
Busload of faith to get by, busload of faith to get by
(Lou Reed, © 1989)

The past two or three years have been a disastrous period for the reputation of North American evangelical and mainline Christianity. Several notorious incidents of prominent tumbles from grace have cluttered the ecclesiastical landscape.

Rumours of an emerging scandal at world-famous Willow Creek Church in Chicago's northwest suburbs were confirmed early in 2018 (Brackear Pashman and Coen, 2018). Allegations of sexual improprieties against women committed by the church's well-known founding pastor, Bill Hybels, became public knowledge. What made the reports particularly onerous was that a team of Hybels' former colleagues, including women he is alleged to have acted inappropriately toward, eventually went to the mainstream media with their stories (Goodstein, 2018). This came about after the church's elders waffled with respect to investigating complaints in accordance with proper standards of protocol (Ortberg, 2018).

By mid-August that year, as various evangelical leaders began to go public with calls for a genuinely independent investigation at Willow Creek, the entire leadership team—including the new co-pastors—had resigned (Silets, 2018). In early September, an outside panel was commissioned to conduct a thorough evaluation of the predatory environment that had prevailed at Willow Creek leading up to the inflammatory controversy. The investigation later reported that the allegations against Hybels were credible (McFarlan Miller, 2019). A reconciliation service held July 23, 2019, was reportedly less than satisfactory (Roys, 2019) and left many questions unanswered (Speight, 2019). Charges of a cover-up ensued (Bedell, 2019).

2018 also brought news of yet more scandal involving American Catholics. Following a 2015 Best Picture Academy Award for the movie *Spotlight* which chronicled reports of rampant sexual abuse by Catholic priests against altar-boys in the archdiocese of Boston during the later years of the twentieth century, more ominous revelations emerged.

Headlines appeared in mid-summer of an enquiry that revealed bishops and other leaders of the Roman Catholic Church in Pennsylvania had covered up child sexual abuse by more than 300 priests in that state over a period of 70 years. The study covered six of Pennsylvania's eight Catholic dioceses and identified more than 1,000 victims. It was the broadest examination to date by a government agency in the U.S. concerning sexual abuse of children in the Catholic Church. Among the heinous acts uncovered, as reported by the *New York Times*, were "a priest who raped a young girl in the hospital after she had her tonsils out … and another priest who was allowed to stay in ministry after impregnating a young girl and arranging for her to have an abortion" (Goodstein and Otterman, 2018).

The late Canadian expatriate and prominent international apologist/evangelist, Ravi Zacharias (d. May 2020), of suburban Atlanta based Ravi Zacharias International Ministries (RZIM) continued to

Chapter Two: Busload of GRACE to Get By

garner criticism throughout 2018. A book was published regarding misleading representations he had allegedly been making for several years about his academic credentials and service. Extensive research led to this frank assessment by San Francisco based lawyer and the book's author, Steve Baughman: "What we see in Mr. Zacharias's self-preservation over the past 35 years is a very clear pattern and practice of deception. These may seem like strong words, but there is a preserved written record that confirms that, sadly, this is exactly what happened" (Rauser, 2018). Word of an inappropriate "sexting" relationship between Zacharias and a married Canadian woman this writer has spoken with numerous times resulted in an undisclosed financial settlement in late 2017 (Shellnutt and Zylstra, 2017).

Additional questions regarding Zacharias's character emerged in the late summer of 2020 following his death from cancer in May of that year. Canadian seminary professor, Randal Rauser, posted a number of blog entries containing and related to a video clip of Steve Baughman in which the latter outlined new allegations that Zacharias had used massage spas under his ownership to exploit women for his own sexual gratification (Rauser, 2020). Rauser also posted a statement by an unidentified "Christian leader" who claimed to have thoroughly investigated the sexual misconduct allegations against Zacharias and said he found them to be credible.

American investigative journalist Julie Roys elaborated with additional posts concerning Zacharias's *modus operandi* with respect to the incident referred to above involving a Canadian woman (Roys, 2020). Discouragingly enough, as of this writing it appears an internationally renowned Christian apologist and his corporate ministry ostensibly devoted to contending for truth was and is intent on avoiding truth when it came to Zacharias's personal moral credibility.

In early December of 2018 the *Fort Worth Star-Telegram* published in-depth coverage of over 400 allegations of sexual abuse in independent fundamentalist Baptist Churches in the U.S. (Smith,

2018). The Southern Baptist Convention was rocked by a six-part revelation of sexual abuse among its churches and missions board that was published beginning February 10, 2019 in the *Houston Chronicle* (Downen, Olsen and Tedesco, 2019). Such news proved sufficient to disgust even the most nominal of believers.

As if such an inventory alone was not enough bad news, you can add to it the details regarding various forms of abuse by pastors at prominent American mega-churches in Chicago and Memphis. Independent Chicago journalist Julie Roys and others have been doggedly documenting the never-ending debacle surrounding (Canadian-born) Pastor James MacDonald's empire at Harvest Bible Chapel in Chicagoland via magazine articles (Roys, 2019), blog-sites (McAlpine, n.d.; Misek, 2018), and podcasts (Roys, 2019). In the summer of 2020, another evangelical megachurch pastor, John Ortberg, cited above with respect to the Bill Hybels scandal, departed his pastorate in suburban San Francisco under a cloud following an enquiry with respect to covering for his own son who admitted to being sexually attracted to children. Reports had circulated for months that Ortberg nonetheless permitted the young man to continue working with children at the church (Roys, 2020).

When placed alongside ongoing public support for controversial American president Donald Trump from prominent evangelical personalities such as Franklin Graham, Robert Jeffress and Jerry Falwell, Jr., the disgrace being heaped upon the Church by its purported leaders became oppressive. If nothing else it lent a certain grassroots-level credibility to evangelical historian Mark Noll's popular contention that "The scandal of the evangelical mind is that there is not much of an evangelical mind…American evangelicals are not exemplary for their thinking, and they have not been so for several generations" (Noll, 1994). With respect to their curious ongoing support of Trump, it is as if American evangelicals are signalling that their myopic understanding of The Great Commission directs: "Go ye therefore and aggressively apply lipstick to a pig in hope that no one will discern your implicit endorsement of the famous Machiavellian ethic that the end justifies the means."

Ostensibly, so passionate are many American evangelicals regarding the issues of abortion and homosexuality—or is such largely a convenient covering for old-fashioned racism in response to the Obama presidency?—that the prospect of reversing legislation on those two inflammatory social matters fully justifies their political support for a man with a well-documented record of misogyny, sexual immorality and dubious business ethics. Or as American journalist Katherine Stewart perceptively indicts:

> Christian nationalists and their allies continue to stand behind the most corrupt, divisive, and chaotic president in history because they believe that he can supply, via the courts, the abortion ban that they see as a necessary prelude to making America a righteous nation again. (Stewart, 2019)

As the months passed, I soon had my fill of the latest "Can-you-believe-this?" headline coming from what I call "American religitics." ("Religitics" is a term I coined to account for the curious hybrid of religion and politics that has influenced my perception of American identity since my childhood given that I grew up with as many American neighbours and classmates as Canadian friends. Apart from "that papist" John F. Kennedy and "that liberal" Lyndon B. Johnson, presidents Eisenhower, Nixon—at least up until Watergate when, or so I was informed, the media sabotaged his presidency!—and Ford were all respectable, God-fearing, church-attending, conservative Christians.) Dartmouth historian Randall Balmer's use of "Religious Right" and Katherine Stewart's employment of "Christian nationalism" are far and away the better-known terms for this dynamic that I call "religitics." (see Balmer, 2006 and Stewart, 2019)

Accordingly, I turned to the balm of popular music—something that has frequently helped keep me professionally afloat during periods of frustrated despondency in pastoral life—seeking solace for my tortured soul.

I had not yet had opportunity to listen to aging rocker Bob Seger's latest album *I Knew You When* (Seger, 2017) so was delighted to find that it contained a cover of the late Lou Reed's hit from thirty years ago that is cited at the beginning of this chapter. As I listened, I found myself tapping the REPEAT key as it slowly occurred to me that there is something of theological significance to be gleaned by changing just one word in Reed's lyrics. From the documentation of the conduct of "God's people" in both the book of Genesis and ongoing into the evangelical world of the 21st century as I have noted, it is certain that if we need a busload of *faith* to get by in life, it is also legitimate to maintain that we need a busload of *grace* to get by in attempting to account for the incongruities involved in mankind's attempts to pursue the life of faith.

Working through a stack of CDs during this period, I also came across my friend Martyn Joseph's insightful hit *It's Not a Good Time for God* (Joseph, 2012). As the astute Welsh crooner conveys, we live in days when, by virtue of their abysmal conduct, many of God's purported spokespeople are certainly not doing the Almighty any public relations favours.

When I pause to consider that many modern, multi-million dollar, so-called "ministries" are being operated these days more like family businesses passed on from father to sons or grandsons, I am hardly surprised to observe that "business as usual" often leads to moral or fiduciary misconduct in such entities. Frederick Buechner hits the bull's eye with his prophetic observation: "there is perhaps no better proof for the existence of God than the way year after year he survives the way his professional friends promote him" (Buechner, 1988).

It is not surprising then that I frequently need the tranquilizing perspectives of wise counselors like Buechner and Will Willimon when the latter writes in a parallel spirit:

> ...[I]n church Jesus makes us put up with one another even as our Lord puts up with us (Eph. 4:2). Flannery O'Connor said that she was happily Catholic because when she went to Mass at her little parish in Manhattan, she always saw a few people she knew—and many more whom she thanked God she didn't know. Like the blind man healed by Jesus (Mark 8:24), it takes a while to move from seeing people as trees walking to looking at them as beloved members of the body of Christ. (Willimon, p. 78)

Regrettably, the sad scenarios I have presented here from church life in North America reflect only a sampling of numerous similar failures that take place with increasing regularity involving lesser known personalities in local churches and Christian ministries. If our politicians are renowned for giving late-night TV comedians no shortage of fodder for their scripts, the ecclesiastical world seems aggressively bent on providing ever more than sufficient scandal to increasingly cynical viewers.

The emergence of grace in Genesis

Discussions today regarding the topic of divine grace are often carried out with prevailing references made to the New Testament portion of the Bible. Many students of Judeo-Christian theology in North America have historically insisted on a radical cleavage between the focus on Law (Hebrew: *Torah*) in the Old Testament and the overwhelming presence of grace (Greek: *charis*) in the New.

While I respect and am conversant with this orientation to the study of Scripture, my lifelong engagement with what I call "parish theology" leads me to avoid maintaining much affinity for such an approach. Rather, and at the risk of agitating some of my friends who are experts in systematic theology, I am resolute in suggesting that grace, the dominant characteristic of God's eternal relationship with mankind, is launched in the very first chapters of the very first book in the Old Testament, Genesis, and endures through to the very last book of the New Testament, Revelation.

In no way do I mean to in any way minimize what the New Testament has to say about grace, as if such is even possible. Rather, and it bears repeating, I am chiefly concerned here to emphasize the fact that, contrary to what many church-goers may have been and are continuing to be led to believe, the Old Testament is *NOT* exclusively concerned with the keeping of the Law or the *Torah* as the basis for a relationship with God. In my estimation, let there be no obscurity about it: the Old Testament prominently evidences the jaw-dropping grace of God right from its opening pages.

I applaud the way pastor and author Brian Zahnd helps to substantiate and augment a most important emphasis to be engaged when comparing what can also be referred to as the Old and New Covenants:

> We have grown accustomed to thinking that the Old Covenant is a covenant based on works, while the New Covenant is based on grace. We think the Old Covenant is legalism and the New Covenant is grace. This is almost entirely false. The Jewish people living under the Covenant of Sinai and the Law of Moses were keenly aware that their sins were forgiven by the grace and mercy of God and not by the merit of their works. The difference between the two covenants is not law and grace. The essential difference between the old and new covenants is this—The New Covenant invites **the whole world** to become God's people. In Christ the chosen people are now the human race and the holy land is the whole earth ... The covenant that began with Abraham and Moses culminated in Christ. In Christ the nations are invited to join God's new covenant, new household, new temple, new Israel, new humanity ... The "new thing" about the New Covenant is that it erases all ethnic, gender, social, political and

class privilege ... Salvation is a kind of belonging! A belonging that was restricted in the Old Covenant, but has now been opened wide in the New Covenant." (Zahnd, 2016, pp. 41–43) (emphasis original)

It is a truth worth unconstrained celebration that, first and foremost, God has ever related to humankind on the basis of grace. That dance-worthy reality protrudes prominently throughout Genesis. The circle of grace, which may be considered comparatively small at the beginning of the Old Testament, is revealed to expand and become ever more inclusive as the Scripture unfolds.

Readers are encouraged to bear in mind that we normally do not begin reading a book by digesting the contents of the last few chapters in order to help us better comprehend those that come first. When the Bible is read from front to back as we in the Western world usually read any book, it is evident that ripples of grace emerge very early in its pages. As we progress in reading through the Old Testament and then the entire Bible, those ripples are transformed into a sustaining swell that is sufficient to buoy the whole of humanity.

Old Testament scholar Sam Mikolaski once wrote: "Grace means that God is determined to accomplish his good and righteous purpose" (Pinnock, (Ed.), 1975, p. 22). The definition attached to "grace" by Mikolaski is pragmatic for my purposes because even a hasty scan of the first chapters of Genesis reveals that God was acting in the creation narrative with a distinct purpose in mind. The earth as we know it and all that was placed in it was brought into being according to the purpose of God for the purpose of God.

Regardless of how one chooses to interpret the Garden of Eden account, it is apparent that God has a purpose for his prohibition to the garden's human occupants about eating from the tree of life. Upon their failure to obey his initial directive, another dimension of his sovereign plan appears in seminal form in Genesis 3:15 where God advises the serpent that he will "put enmity between you and the woman, and between your offspring and hers; he will crush your head and you will strike his heel."

Here we see the wisdom found in the simple observation that "Grace is God in his givenness" (Buechner, 2006, p. 178). Despite the complications posed by mankind's free will and the evidence of God's dismay at human obstinacy, God continues to give because giving was at the core of his person and his purpose as devised before the foundations of the world.

The term for "grace" or "favour" (Hebrew: *hen*) first occurs in what becomes the flood narrative when we are told (Genesis 6:5ff) that the Lord saw how great man's wickedness on the earth had become and that every inclination of the thoughts of man's heart was evil all the time. It is in this ominous context that verse 8 states: "but Noah found favour/grace (Hebrew: *hen*) in the eyes of the Lord."

Victor P. Hamilton's insights provide essential clarification at this point with respect to how God's interaction with humankind originates from his attribute of "giving" or as noted above, what Frederick Buechner calls "his givenness:"

> Most translations of the Bible have Noah "finding" favour with Yahweh. A few (e.g., NEB) have Noah "winning" favour with Yahweh. There is a significant difference between the two. The former denotes no moral quality on the part of the person who is designated as having found favour. On these grounds Noah's election would be just that, and no causal relationship should be seen between Noah's finding favour (vs. 8) and his character (vs. 9).
>
> The latter option "winning favour" shows a nexus between the two verses, with the line of argumentation being effect to cause (i.e., substantiation) rather than cause to effect (i.e., causation). Of course had the order of the two verses been switched, there would have been no doubt that Noah's righteousness and blamelessness were intended to supply a

> rationale for his election and escape from the Flood. If we translate Heb. "hen" as "grace" instead of "favour," then further support for "finding" is available. Grace is found or received, not won.
>
> The phrase "find favour in the one's eyes" occurs a number of times in Genesis with a wealth of nuances that cannot be captured by one English equivalent. Thus, 18:3, "My lord, if I may beg of you this favour;" 19:19, "if you would but indulge your servant;" 32:5; 33:8; "in the hope of gaining your favour;" 39:7, "he took a fancy to." (Hamilton, 1996, p. 276)

Let me again be clear with respect to the considered assumption behind how I am using the term and concept of "grace" throughout this book. To emphasize Hamilton again on the matter: "Grace is **found or received, not won**" (emphasis added). The importance of this component of grace's DNA cannot be overstated and will become increasingly obvious as we proceed story by story in Genesis.

Against this brief but crucial background, it is appropriate to now bring in a New Testament flavour to augment the definition of "grace" as I understand the term and employ it in the thinking behind my work. Vernon C. Grounds suggests:

> [Grace] is God's utterly inscrutable attitude of mercy and kindness which motivates His self-sacrifice in Jesus Christ, a redemptive action for which no reason can be assigned. Contradicting and nullifying all norms of logic and justice, grace offers forgiveness and reconciliation where wrath and exile are properly merited. (Pinnock, (Ed.), p. 23)

To this, W.H. Griffith-Thomas, further elucidates: "Grace is, first, a quality of graciousness in the Giver, and then, a quality of gratitude in the recipient, which in turn makes him gracious to those around" (Ibid., p. 24).

I, therefore, define grace as the kindness of God initiated before the world to be ultimately gifted through Jesus Christ to people of the Creator's choosing for His purposes alone with no account whatsoever of the recipient's merit or lack thereof. In the big picture, let us be certain, grace says far more about the nature of the Giver than it does about the nature of the receiver. In sum, we now come back to where we began this book by making reference to Rick Warren's astute assertion: "It's not about you."

Amazing grace is also "amusing" grace

As we will frequently see throughout our review of Genesis, observing the grace of God at work in the life of human beings can be as amusing as it is amazing.

I advance this notion because grace—"unmerited favour" or "undeserved kindness," the foundational and traditional definition I am employing for the Hebrew word "*hen*" (and related) and the Greek word "*charis*" (and related) as discussed in these pages—is, as Genesis reveals, extended to and obtained by people whose qualifications for receiving such are often, at best, a bad joke.

Philip Yancey aptly captures the subtle humour of this sobering notion when he states:

> Grace means **there is nothing we can do to make God love us more**—no amount of spiritual callisthenics and renunciations, no amount of knowledge gained from seminaries or divinity schools, no amount of crusading on behalf of righteous causes. And grace means **there is nothing we can do to make God love us less**—no amount of racism or pride or pornography or adultery or even murder. Grace means that God already loves us as much as an infinite God can possibly love. (Yancey, 1997, p. 70) (emphasis added)

If ever there was a sentiment that conflicts with the realities that govern North American culture in the twenty-first century, this is it.

Yancey's studied suggestion, therefore, merits repeating: "there is **nothing** we can do to make God love us more ... and there is **nothing** we can do to make God love us less." (emphasis added)

Adequately comprehending that grace functions counter-intuitively to what we are regularly told and experience in the course of everyday life is truly a head-scratcher. Eventually, however, it becomes more than sufficient cause for a smile, and yes, for even audible and prolonged laughter. That is because such a notion strikes us not only as being entirely foreign to our human frame of reference but also as being far, far too good to be true.

Is it not an underlying principle of our daily experience that what we *do* is of primary importance not only with regard to how others respond to us but as to what we accomplish in life? Numerous popular idioms capture this reality. "No pain—no gain." "Early to bed, early to rise, makes a man healthy, wealthy and wise." "If at first you don't succeed, try, try again." And so forth.

Pleasing our parents is perhaps the first exposure we receive to grasping this elemental premise of the human experience informing us that how we behave has a definite impact on how people will respond to us. When we enter pre-school, kindergarten and elementary school, we begin a life-long education in the fact that how we conduct ourselves largely determines not only the way others respond to us but how our efforts to succeed are received. The same holds true with regard to refraining from doing certain actions. This relational dynamic is also a fundamental lesson underscored in the quest to find friends, in the training one pursues for a career, in obtaining a domestic partner and in the course of climbing the ladder of success in one's chosen vocation.

In sum, then, the governing principle of life as engrained in us from infancy is: prove yourself worthy by virtue of what you do or do not do! Our rewards in life are largely dependent on our adherence to this overarching rule.

It is hardly a surprise, then, that many of us truly struggle throughout life to fully understand let alone accept the idea that when it comes to a relationship with God, a different construct altogether governs that liaison.

Whoa! Let's slow down just a moment.

Do I mean to tell you that there is nothing you or I can do for better or worse to in any way influence God's attitude and action toward us? That's right! The ability to truly absorb such a reality requires some major reorientation to our usual pattern of thinking, correct?

Hear it again, then, to accentuate it. Am I saying the paradigm that governs our interaction in our relationship with the Divine is 180 degrees different from any other relationship we will ever have in life? Indeed, I am.

So, okay, what is the catch because, surely, there has to be one?

The reason we even surmise that there is a "catch" is because of our standard experiences in life. You usually get what you deserve. We have learned to accept that reality. Now, however, we are in territory that requires us to be comfortable with unfamiliarity, something that is far easier said than done.

We are casually aware, of course, that the underlying marvel that constitutes the essence of the Christian gospel is that God has this inclination to offer his very best to the very worst. When framed in the context of the terminology I have chosen to employ in this book, another way of identifying the humour inherent in the miracle of grace is to note that God has a long history when it comes to turning losers into winners. The truth is that God has always known that turning losers into winners would require something that losers are entirely incapable of providing.

The old hymn *Rock of Ages* perhaps says it best in this regard: "Nothing in my hand I bring, simply to thy cross I cling; naked, come to thee for dress; helpless, look to thee for grace."

It may be necessary here for me to clarify that a meaningful engagement of Holy Week every year graphically reminds us that, indeed, there is nothing remotely humorous about the cross of Calvary which enabled God to extend the gift of grace to "wretches" or "worms" like ourselves. (In his famous hymn, *Amazing Grace*, John Newton wrote: "Amazing grace, how sweet the sound; that saved a wretch like me." Isaac Watts in his well-known hymn, *At the Cross*, wrote "Alas, and did my Saviour bleed, and did my Sov'reign die? Would he devote that sacred head, for such a worm as I?" More recent versions of Watts' hymn substitute: "Would he devote that sacred head, for sinners such as I?") (A nod of the head at this point is due those of you who still don't like my employment of the word "loser." May the Almighty grant you grace in your hour of turmoil!) We are gravely mistaken should we fail to remember, to borrow from Dietrich Bonhoeffer's classic treatment of the topic, that it is a *costly* grace that is justifiably accessible to the fallen, the broken, the wounded and the sinful (Bonhoeffer, 1963).

Some readers will be aware that various theologians of a Calvinistic predilection have historically identified mankind's natural and universal condition as "totally depraved." This is truly a harsh designation that nevertheless adds a note of sobriety and, I suggest, may well be necessarily attendant to any adequate theological discussion of the nature of God's grace.

The purpose of this volume, however, is not primarily to expound the unfathomable compassion of the Giver of the gift of grace or to present a compelling definition of the spectacular nature of the gift. I recommend readers to consult the works of others far more articulate than I am on those matters, some of which I have listed at the conclusion of this work (see p. 195).

My focus here, rather, is to endeavour to advance my longstanding appreciation of the immeasurable value of the gift by noting the somewhat amusing nature of the ever-present dysfunctions that have forever been common to the beneficiaries of God's amazing grace.

To repeat, then, I call such people "losers," not to be disrespectful or dismissive of them, but because, like you and me, they were often their own worst enemies when it came to pursuing a life that might be considered remotely worthy of the grace granted them. (Ha. *Worthy*. There it is: a reminder as to how truly difficult it is for us to remove any notion of merit from the receiving end of God's favour). "Losers" is a term I think fairly captures, at least to some extent, the reputations of so many of the people featured in the earliest pages of The Holy Bible as well as in the religious news arising out of North American Christianity in the twenty-first century.

As explained above, I am convinced that using such terminology as "losers" greatly assists in underscoring the magnitude of God's grace as seen by his relentless commitment to turning losers into winners. So, I state again that I do not hesitate to classify myself a loser. And, having served as a pastor in four congregations over thirty-plus years coupled with some of the embarrassing incidents identified at the start of this chapter, perhaps you will forgive me for the suggestion that the local church is essentially a collection of losers trying to make personal and collective progress in Christian discipleship in an effort to see Christ's kingdom come and his will be done "on earth as it is in heaven" (Matthew 6:10).

I invite you again, therefore, to take a closer look with me at several men and women who were among the original recipients of God's grace in the book of Genesis. We find them going about their lives lying, doubting, conniving, cheating, double-crossing, committing immorality and serving their self-interests first. In short, we encounter them demonstrating their bankruptcy of merit, their foreignness to favour and how exquisitely undeserving they were. They generally carried on like the sordid fare we self-righteous types associate with the values dispensed today via soap operas, reality TV and much of what comes out of Hollywood.

I think it is worth a chuckle or two or three that such losers are nonetheless presented to us as the emerging "people of God." For the truth is that they were men and women chosen by God to play a strategic role in establishing his community on earth and accomplishing his purposes in this world.

So are we.

They were seriously flawed personalities to whom God—get this—was willing, at least to some extent, to affix his own reputation.

So are we.

And THAT, I contend, is both amazing and amusing.

Engaging the perspectives behind this study

I wish to identify at this point the main perspectives I have implemented in this review of several prominent personalities portrayed in Genesis. I encourage readers to employ them as well.

I believe it will be beneficial for you as you again read these stories to keep these tenets in mind and put them to work on your own behalf. Not only am I hopeful my approach will help you develop a more realistic perspective regarding these Biblical characters, but that it will also assist you in trying to cope with and properly engage the public failings of modern faith leaders as documented at the beginning of this chapter.

> 1. Allow the story or incident to speak for itself with no attempt to soften or legitimize it to make it more palatable to the theological convictions or prejudices we hold as members of a culture long removed from the period in focus. In this Netflix era, try and read the Biblical texts I give you as one episode or as a series of episodes in a particular "season" of the lives of the characters presented.

This will require you to discipline yourself to be alert to any conscious or unconscious tendencies you may have to manipulate any of the stories reviewed here in order to make them better conform to your theological or cultural preferences or familiarities. Be wary of merely applauding the sovereignty of God or concluding that God moves in mysterious ways to account for the human failings and the divine inexplicabilities on display in the Biblical narrative. Do your best to read the stories for what they are (God's

Word) while employing your imagination in an effort to obtain even an elementary grasp of how the story might have been "spun" by twenty-first century media, religious or mainstream. Remember the shock you experienced when you first heard about the moral failure of a respected religious leader in your circles? Don't minimize or dismiss the shock value of these ancient stories simply because you are convinced we do not fully understand ancient times or because you think "I've heard everything now" by virtue of the sordid times in which we live.

> 2. Consciously avoid the inclination most of us have somehow acquired to see the characters of Genesis as people of moral or spiritual superiority to ourselves.

The one trait that all human beings have in common is that they are human beings. Abraham, Sarah, Isaac, Rebekah, Jacob and the others considered here therefore represent aspects of the best and the worst of human nature. They are not worthy of elevation merely because they appear in the narrative of Scripture. While there is indeed much to be learned from their positive traits and behaviours, there is equally as much education to be found in the vivid depictions we are given of their being fully susceptible to human failings.

I unapologetically encourage you to be inspired by their failures, emboldened by their mistakes and instructed by the prominence given to the abundant evidence of their being fully human.

> 3. Bear in mind that God chose to initially "grace" these people with his call to or his selection of them while being fully aware of human depravity in general and of the specific failing(s) to which each of these figures would eventually succumb.

If, as many of us affirm, God knows all things and is sovereign, it follows that God never had any "if I'd only known" moments when confronted with the undeniable evidence of wrongdoing by his chosen servant(s). Whether we like it or not or can adequately explain it or not, apart from the challenging interpretation of the assertion of Genesis 6:6,7 that "The Lord was grieved that he had made man on the earth, and his heart was filled with pain....so I will wipe mankind...from the face of the earth...for I am grieved that I have made them," there is minimal evidence throughout Genesis that God ever had second thoughts about choosing, calling or blessing Abraham and his lineage. For better or worse, God determined to engage and bless fallible human beings, and to assume all the associated risks to his reputation in so doing. And he still does so today. (See #5 in this list for an additional connection to this line of thought).

> 4. As best you can, try and read the Biblical texts associated with each of these figures as if you were reading such for the first time and as if you know nothing of what follows with respect to that individual in subsequent Scripture. For example, we know little about Abraham prior to being introduced to him in Genesis 12. Therefore, make an effort to not allow the statement of Genesis 15:6 that "Abraham believed the Lord, and he credited it to him as righteousness" or of St. Paul's Romans 4 discussion of Abraham's righteousness to unduly "colour" your grasp of how self-absorbed Abraham was in the last half of Genesis 12 and again in Genesis 20.

Supply some effort to disassociate from the "and they all lived happily ever after" kind of thinking as you read the Biblical texts. Strive to get into the stories as the original husband, wife, mother, father, older son, younger daughter, *et cetera*, would have seen, heard or felt what transpires, or as the broader community of faith in these stories would have been forced to do. For example, what did Sarah think of Abraham's insistence that she lie to the Egyptians about her identity? She outright laughed at the divine visitors' assertion that she would give birth at her advanced age, so there is some evidence that she was not just a passive, submissive woman willing to unquestioningly take whatever her husband dished out. Attempt to insert yourself into the "flow" of the narrative as you read and monitor what kind of emotions, thoughts, questions might have come to you had you been present centuries ago to watch and experience the dysfunction, deceit and wrongdoing unfold.

> 5. Be sure to take note of the comparative lack of evidence in the text of any divine judgment/ punishment or what we might call "consequences" for the blatant moral failings of God's people as featured in Genesis. In some instances, the perpetrators or the guilty in these episodes appear to emerge scot-free from any rebuke from God or in terms of any detriment to God's plan or further use of or blessing on them. In others, God is more interested in blessing than faulting wrongdoers. What are we to make of such realities?

Take the story of Jacob as an example of what I am underscoring in this regard. After deviously outsmarting his older brother and his aging father, Jacob is forced to "hit the road, Jac" upon learning of Esau's intent to kill him. Fleeing for his life to go and live with Uncle Laban (whom he then undertakes to also "rip-off"), God appears to Jacob in a dream one night. Decent people might think that the least God might have done was to give Jacob a stern, verbal rebuke for the behaviour the latter had just visited on his father and brother. But no. God does not direct one word of correction to Jacob, later to be named Israel. There is not even a disciplinary cuff upside the head and "you need to make some improvements in your behaviour, Jacob, if you expect me to bless you" from the Almighty. All that occurs is a reaffirmation from God that Jacob will be blessed.

Attempt to get your head around this attribute of the God of Genesis. He appears "locked in" or, we might say, almost "forced" to bless Abraham's grandson because of a promise made years before to Grandpa Abe. The theological and ethical implications (see #8) of this reality are very significant and, although I have chosen to not address such to any depth in this book, are certainly of relevance to any discussion concerning how the modern day Church disciplines and otherwise deals with the moral failings of its leaders.

> 6. As you read, bear in mind the words of Jesus in Matthew 7:3: "Why do you look at the speck of sawdust in your brother's eye and pay no attention to the plank in your own eye?" Most of us find it much easier to identify the glaring faults and sins in others while minimizing our own. To observe only the shortcomings of the ancients without using them to seriously consider our own spiritual failures and weaknesses might be educational but it's comparatively myopic in terms of achieving any personal spiritual growth.

We are all aware of the relative ease with which we can identify wrongdoing in the lives of others all the while minimizing, ignoring or even failing to see our own obtrusive failures. The book of Genesis might well be considered a mirror or a looking glass that offers us the gift necessary to engage the warning of St. James (1:22, 23) regarding the folly of the one who "looks at his face in a mirror and, after looking at himself, goes away and immediately forgets what he looks like."

Twenty-first century society and particularly the Church therein do not need more people who know truth but do not live truth. This book will fail in its objective if all it accomplishes is conveying additional information to you to be stock-piled in a life that is pockmarked with spiritual inconsistencies. And I am looking at myself in the mirror when I make that statement.

7. As you review the details of these ancient stories, allow yourself to consciously identify and release any inclination you may detect to feeling like you have to defend God's action OR inaction in terms of his response or lack thereof to the failings of his chosen people.

One of the weaknesses of the evangelical community as I have experienced it in my life is a holdover from its historical affinity with fundamentalism. I am speaking here of what I would call an unhealthy obsession with orthodoxy to the point of feeling that we have to defend, explain or otherwise try to justify God's behaviour whenever either his actions or inactions do not quite square with our systematic theology's propositional statements regarding some component of his character.

No, we don't. There is minimal evidence in Scripture that believers are called to be apologists for why God does or does not do what God does or does not do. Our compulsion in this regard has more to do with modern evangelicalism's love affair with scientific rationalism than with anything else. God has been doing quite well for himself or herself since long before you or I came along to try and defend or explain him or her.

Let me attempt to enlighten the point this way. Years ago, esteemed evangelical theologian-philosopher Francis Schaeffer penned a philosophical treatise concerning the existence of God titled *He is There and He Is Not Silent* (Schaeffer, 1972). The relatively brief essay very competently made its case regarding God's existence and the ample evidence for such.

However, as we will see repeatedly in the stories of Genesis and as I have witnessed numerous times as a pastor while engaging people who are experiencing the demanding challenges associated with being human, it is also true that God often is and is perceived by his followers as definitely being silent when it comes to our imperfect human attempts to detect his presence and activity in our lives.

Don't take my word for this. That is the reason we have Scriptural laments such as Psalm 13 and Habakkuk where God's seeming disappearance, inactivity or complete lack of concern or awareness is bemoaned by the writers of God's Word. The reality of the human experience is that owing to God's silence, sometimes we simply do not sense that God is there or is even remotely interested in what is going on in our lives.

Fathers of Christendom such as Thomas Aquinas (1225–1274) used the Latin term *Deus Absconditus* to describe this "hiddenness" of God. We, of course, derive the English term "abscond" from this concept. To abscond is to depart in a sudden or secret manner often in the interests of avoiding capture or legal prosecution. Believers have always had to grapple with the perception that at times God seems to have hidden himself or to have taken himself out of the picture leaving us with no small amounts of angst and consternation.

God is God which, by definition, means he does not have to explain his or her ways to anyone for anything s/he does or does not do. God's primary function in this world is not to conduct himself in a manner whereby we can then bolster or amend our systematic theology so that it provides us with the "warm fuzzies" we may believe we need in order to spiritually survive. Trust me, there will be times in life when the best we can come up with to try and explain the Almighty's activity or inactivity is to affirm that God is God and let the theological crumbs fall where they may.

8. As you engage the stories of the different characters considered in this book, bear in mind that the matter of reconciling Old Testament ethics with a larger Judeo-Christian worldview remains a complex and evolving field of study. Much as some of us may not like it, the fact is that such continues to be a "grey area" of Biblical and theological study.

Walter C. Kaiser, Jr., addresses this reality when he states:

> Old Testament morality does have its limitations, however. While contemporary ethicists must take the Old Testament seriously if they are going to properly represent the total canonical contribution to biblical or theological ethics, Old Testament ethics is not the final chapter in the canonical spectrum of concepts. This testament reaches out beyond itself for fulfillment in Jesus Christ and the New Testament. Therefore, it is necessary for us to acknowledge at least four limitations to our discipline... (Kaiser, p. 34)

Keep in mind as you read the Genesis stories that, for whatever reason(s) or combination thereof, it appears the squaring or reconciling of the depraved behaviour of the characters in Genesis with what is frequently referred to as "Judeo-Christian ethics" does not appear to have been a priority at all for the writer(s) of the first book of the Bible. The characters lied, cheated, deceived, because that is what humans do regardless of where they are in their experience of God's unmerited favour. Any theological or ethical tension you may experience in noting this dynamic is not something that the writer(s) of Genesis felt they needed to address or justify whatsoever.

Accordingly, the perspective that I adopt in this book in this regard is similar to that articulated by Kaiser when he notes: "...divine approval of an individual in one aspect or area of his life does not entail and must not be extended to mean that there is a divine approval of that individual in all aspects of his character or conduct" (Ibid., p. 271).

****

"The God of Abraham, Isaac and Jacob" the Scriptures declare in exaltation of the Deity unveiled in Genesis.

Yikes! Those guys? Yes.

Get ready to roll your eyes along with me and articulate something like this as you read. "You mean to say that God purposely and consciously allowed himself to be associated with these rascals, ne'er-do-wells, shysters and losers?"

Seriously!?

Yes!

To emphasize, then, for a combination of reasons, some of which I have already identified, many North American fundagelicals have piously elevated these Biblical figures to a position where they are considered, if not our own version of "patron saints," then definitely that of a venerated "father" or "mother" of the Christian faith. In so doing, at times we have chosen to overlook the glaring reality that they were fallible folks just like us who had many days that likely found them saying or thinking, "I can't believe I just did or said that!"

You know exactly what I am talking about, don't you? I am referring to those days that found them accusing themselves: "Dude, Girl, you are such a spiritual loser!" Yes, just like them, we know only too well that were God to send us a text message today, it would frequently include the "eye-roll" or the "smack-my-forehead" emoticon.

The conspicuous fallibility of these saints is a truth I have come to see as not only most reassuring of God's patience with me, but truly as amusing as it is amazing. I am confident that once you have viewed these heroes of the faith through the lens I incorporate in these pages, you will want to laugh out loud next time you are able to identify that you have just "pulled an Abraham" or "a Rebekah" or "a Jacob" in your own walk in grace.

So laugh along with me not so much to excuse yourself as to celebrate the amazing and amusing grace of the God who, for his own purposes alone, chose to reach out and put his hand on your shoulder as an expression of his desire to be in relationship with you. As you read, I hope you will encounter an even greater amazement at God's inexplicable kindness not only in initially gracing you, but in continuing to grace you despite the numerous reminders all of us regularly encounter regarding how far we have yet to go in terms of getting it all together.

In so doing, I am very confident that by the time you finish reading the book, you will be in agreement with me regarding the suggestion that we all need a busload of GRACE to get by.

Chapter Three:
My Name is Abraham, and I am a Liar
(Genesis 12:1–13:4)

Sometimes I think that Jesus watches my neurotic struggles, and shakes his head and grips his forehead and starts tossing back mojitos.
(Anne Lamott, 2007, p. 56)

Adherents of the world's primary monotheistic religions—Christianity, Islam and Judaism—all revere Abraham as a father of their respective faiths. Christians are certainly aware that the New Testament speaks of this ancient gentleman in a most favourable light. Abraham is presented to us as an enduring example of saving faith in Romans 4 and Hebrews 11. Accordingly, he is among those Biblical figures many of us were trained as children to admire and emulate with respect to taking the risk of obeying God's guidance in our lives without any hesitation whatsoever.

But wait a minute. Having reviewed the story in the text noted above, surely it is appropriate for modern readers to press the PAUSE button and ask a few questions concerning this guy's behaviour immediately after he is introduced to us. Add to the mix that a similar incident appears in chapter 20 of Genesis. (There are a variety of perspectives among the commentators as to how the chapter 20 story relates to this one and/or how a similar disgrace committed by Isaac in chapter 26 is to be understood in regard to these. It is not within the scope of this work to thoroughly engage those matters but simply note the existence of the various incidents and the similarity in behaviour between father and son).

Whatever questions we might ask with respect to Abraham's actions in this narrative are shared by most scholars. Speculation regarding why Abraham does what he does is widespread but solid answers are few. This reality is evident in Hamilton's treatment of the scenario:

> Why did Abram feel constrained to resort to deception? How different is the Abram of 12:10–20 from the trusting, obedient Abram of 12:1–9! Could it be that he acts, however, despicably, in order to keep alive the promises of God that he had recently received? It is impossible for God to make of Abram a great nation if Abram is dead before he fathers one child. How can God give Canaan to Abram's seed if he has no seed? To prevent such a possibility, Abram must do all he can to stay alive. He is giving Yahweh a little assistance in a potentially embarrassing situation! Here is the first threat to the realization of God's promises: a dead Abram, dead either through starvation or through execution. (Hamilton, p. 383)

As the quotation from Karen Armstrong in Chapter One indicates, those of us who come from traditions conversant with what are commonly referred to as North American family values might be excused for being somewhat perplexed by this particular anecdote from Abraham's life. It hardly seems consistent with our convictions as to what should be the proper conduct of a husband who claims keen allegiance to God.

Some of you are probably familiar with a popular evangelical Christian men's movement that started in the late twentieth century and swept across our continent known as Promise Keepers (PK). For more than twenty-five years now, the organization has conducted large and small men's rallies and published various materials encouraging scores of Christian men in North America to take more initiative with respect to what PK considers is their God-given responsibility to be more godly husbands and fathers.

Chapter Three: My Name is Abraham, and I am a Liar

In this account from Genesis, Abraham does not present a good example of the kind of thinking or conduct that Promise Keepers promotes. If you are or ever have been an evangelical Christian parent, male or female, please think critically with me about Abraham's actions at this point in his life.

Would you be comfortable with your daughter marrying and moving off to God knows where with a man of Abraham's moral fibre as reflected in this incident? I can only imagine the conversation that ensued when Sarah advised her parents of her imminent relocation. "You're taking our darling daughter where, Abraham? What? You do not know where? Well, can you at least make a guarantee to us that she will be safe?"

Had they only known.

Or let's alter the perspective a bit. If you are a North American Christian woman or wife, can you truly say you would be content in a marriage to a man who treats you in accordance with how Abraham treated Sarah in this story? Be honest now, ladies. Is this the kind of conduct you envisioned back there on your wedding day when your husband promised to love, honour and cherish you?

What bizarre malady had overtaken Abraham leading him to cuddle up to such dishonesty? Lewis Smedes creatively captures the nuance when he projects:

> I can imagine Sarah waking up about four in the morning, hearing the bustling noises of Abraham packing. And Sarah says, "What are you doing, Abe?" "Packing." "What for?" "Well, we're leaving." "Where are we going?" "I don't know." "Why are we going?" Because He told me to." "Who's He?" "He didn't tell me." And then I could imagine Sarah calling her father: "What am I going to do?" Her father says, "I knew you shouldn't have married this nut." (Moyers, (Ed.), p. 162–163)

No kidding! Despite retaining some misgivings about this expedition, Sarah nevertheless faithfully—some might say foolishly—follows her visionary husband only to have him quickly reward her by treating her in a manner similar to how he might have bartered his livestock.

Some readers will recall hearing about (although I am confident none of you ever actually saw) the Hollywood movie a few years back titled *Indecent Proposal* that featured Woody Harrelson, Demi Moore and Robert Redford (no spoiler alert is perhaps necessary).

An upwardly mobile married couple, David and Diana Murphy, played by Harrelson and Moore, are doing very well in their respective careers as architect and real estate agent. Until a financial recession sets in, that is, whereupon David loses his lucrative job rendering them unable to continue mortgage payments on their lavish home.

They proceed to borrow $5,000 and head for Las Vegas in hopes of scoring a jackpot or six in the casinos. What starts out well soon turns ugly and it is not long until they are much deeper in debt than when they left home.

Enter billionaire John Gage, played by Robert Redford, who is immediately attracted to the gorgeous Diana and invites the couple to an opulent party at his hotel suite. Gage ends up offering Murphy a million dollars to sleep with the beautiful Diana for just one night thereby presenting the couple with a moral dilemma.

And as for God's chosen servant Abraham—not so much, apparently!

You thought such a scenario was just a concoction of the Wall Street and Hollywood types and indicative of the loose morals rumoured to prevail in those circles, didn't you? You concluded that *Indecent Proposal* was merely a screenplay that originated from some trashy novel, right?

Well, here is a variation of that best-selling story in, of all places, The Holy Bible.

With respect to Abraham's surprising behaviour here, I hasten to remind you of what I stated at the end of Chapter Two about the complicated matter of attempting to reconcile the occasionally vile action(s) of God's selected servants with a larger Judeo-Christian ethic that emerges in the Bible. I do so because I am convinced that it is virtually impossible for modern readers to keep from asking some variation of this question: what could possibly have been going on in Abraham's mind at this point in his life?

We can speculate, but ultimately, we have to try and settle the matter with a perspective that may not be entirely problem free. Walter C. Kaiser, Jr. engages Abraham's antics concerning Sarah's identity in this manner:

> Various attempts have been made to extricate Abraham from the sin and guilt of lying. On two separate occasions he resorted to falsehood as a human expedient to save his beautiful wife from the clutches of lustful monarchs (Gen. 12:10–20; 20:2–18). Twice Abraham lied to Pharaoh and "Abimelech" ... saying, "She [i.e., his wife, Sarah] is my sister" (Gen. 12:13; 20:2).
>
> Now it is true that Sarah was his half-sister, and it is also true that in that culture it was sometimes possible to issue a "sistership contract" along with a marriage contract that then gave the wife greater protection. But it is also obvious that neither of these two nuances were caught by either monarch, if that is what it had intended to produce. Both monarchs complained that they had not been adequately apprised that Sarah was indeed his wife. Thus, while Abraham mightily trusted God in leaving Ur (Gen. 12:1) ... and in being willing to offer Isaac his son (Gen. 22), he certainly was not to be commended in his anxiety over his wife and the ruse he devised to protect her. The tragedy is that Abraham taught his son the same sin, which Isaac then used in Genesis 26:6–11. Again, we repeat with Greene, "Commendation of a character need not imply commendation of every element of the character." (Kaiser, p. 271)

Karen Armstrong is not so accommodating toward Abraham's conduct. She aptly captures the uncomfortable truth facing readers of Genesis when she writes:

> Abraham may have had vision, but he was no paragon. Shortly after we first meet him, we see him engaged in a shady plot to save his own life at the expense of his wife ... Today we often see morality as central to the religious life. The authors of Genesis were certainly interested in ethics, but it was not a primary consideration for them. They do not shrink from presenting the patriarchs in an unfavourable light; they often fail to come up to the moral standards that we would expect to find in a man of God." (Armstrong, pp. 60–61)

What was going on in Abraham's mind here, I previously asked. I think it may have been something along the following speculation which I have learned from reviewing my own failures after the fact.

Approaching Egypt and possibly experiencing serious hunger, given the famine he was fleeing back in Canaan, it occurs to Abraham that he has a significant problem. (I had thought of saying it occurred to him he had some excess baggage—his wife, Sarah. But I have learned the ladies tend to get cranky when I articulate such sparks of wisdom, so I thought better of it).

Abraham's attractive wife, it would appear, had been crowned Beauty Queen of Canaan for several years in succession. She had consistently enhanced her natural beauty by proving herself intelligent and articulate as well. Perhaps of more importance, she was a knock-out when it came to the swimming suit portion of the contest—this was in the days before that component of beauty pageants was cancelled—and the judges were mesmerized as she strolled down the runway in the evening gown competition. In all likelihood, Sarah had graced the covers of most of the *People* magazines of that day and was a frequent guest on *Good Morning, Haran.*

Forced to take his family and entourage to Egypt to survive a deadly famine shortly after but a brief stint in Canaan, Abraham suddenly realizes that when it came to how they interacted with pretty women, the Egyptians had a rather rude reputation with respect to the kind of treatment they extended to husbands. The Egyptians reportedly did not lose any sleep whatsoever before separating a foreigner's head from his torso if that was what was necessary to abduct the attractive Mrs. and present her as a gift to the Pharaoh.

Abraham, therefore, does exactly what both you and I do on a fairly consistent basis: he consults his pocket-sized version of the current best-seller, *It's All About You!* That is, he succumbs to a panic attack over his own prospects for survival and immediately goes to his personal iPod and tunes in Bachman-Turner Overdrive's best-selling hit song, *Lookin' Out for #1* (Bachman-Turner Overdrive, 1975).

Contrary to Hamilton's perspective that I noted, I find minimal indication in the text that Abraham is motivated by a comparatively noble thought such as "my life could be on the line here and then whatever would happen to God's plan to make of me a great nation?" His tactics appear to be entirely self-serving, similar to what surfaces later in the Old Testament when David places Bathsheba's husband, Uzziah, in the front line of battle to conveniently and hastily secure Bathsheba as his wife (2 Samuel 11).

Abraham, God's chosen servant to be the father of a great nation proves to be a self-serving manipulator and liar and we are just nicely into the first chapter of his story. Some example of faith he turns out to be. Without using much imagination at all, I can hear somebody saying, "That's really a brilliant strategy, Abraham. You'll likely survive all right, but I'm afraid we're going to have to cancel you as one of the speakers at the next Focus on the Family conference." Indeed. Abraham is hardly a stellar example of faith and veracity at this point in his record.

Verses 12 and 13 of Genesis 12 present fairly strong evidence that Abraham's primary concern in this predicament was to save his own neck. That's right. Preserving his own welfare at the expense of his wife's virtue was the paramount consideration for this spiritual giant. If Sarah had to compromise her purity and go sleep with the Pharaoh or a few Egyptian pagans in order for him to survive—well, hey, no problem—that could be arranged rather quickly as far as Abraham was concerned.

Again, dedicated evangelical parent, can you conceive of sending your daughter off to some cannibalistic missionary frontier with a guy who demonstrates the morality of this buffoon? Self-centredness. Deceit. Betrayal. Situational ethics. Lying. Each of such nefarious attributes can be identified in the behaviour of this man we best remember, if ever so selectively, for his exemplary faith.

How easy this father of the faith begins to act like a son of a devil leading one to ponder precisely what of any value can be extracted from this debacle. But then again, good lessons can be derived from bad examples. Let us, therefore, attempt to find something instructive arising from this curious and troublesome anecdote.

People of admirable faith can also be people with prominent flaws

Eugene Rivers III points us in the right direction with this comment:

> Abraham's moral ambiguity is an argument for the position that you don't have to be a goody-goody to function as an instrument of God. Like all of us, Abraham is a flawed human being ... I resonate with Abraham, and I identify with his frailty and humanity. I love the fact that from this story I know that an eternal God will be in conversation with the most

> broken, mischievous, pragmatic, and self-centered individual. (Moyers, (Ed.), pp. 157, 170)

Be it an incident from centuries ago or a newspaper article from the twenty-first century, it is a simple fact of history that people of admirable faith can also be people with prominent flaws. To state it another way, very early in its pages the Bible reveals that exemplary faith does not grant immunity to conspicuous behavioural foibles. Fear, doubt and self-preservation can very quickly lead any one of us to commit a major gaffe in judgment thereby compromising our highly prized values.

How is it that a man we find displaying such outstanding and enviable faith at the beginning of Genesis 12 is so swiftly reduced to embracing a self-centred frame of mind that bodes ill for his very own wife? Is it even worthwhile to speculate?

Abraham's DayTimer probably did not have this scenario pencilled in for the day. Inside the pressure cooker of realizing the Egyptians likely had all kinds of plans in mind for Sarah, Abraham senses he is merely an obstacle to their lascivious intent. He was in their way, an inconvenience, a hindrance who simply had to be permanently dispatched so that the king could add another beauty to his harem.

Thus, did fear triumph over faith which soon lead him to failure.

Men, I remind you not to be too harsh in your assessment of Abraham at this point if only because very few of us as husbands have likely found ourselves in comparable circumstances. Be wary of dogmatically maintaining that you would not have been equally paralyzed by fear, gripped by panic, or controlled by circumstance. It is usually far easier to be comforted by a guiding ideology or, perhaps more applicable yet, to be certain of our theological convictions when we are not in the other guy's sandals.

Caught in the squeeze of his circumstances, Abraham appears to either forget or to ignore the spiritual delight he had encountered not that long ago when God had promised to make of him a great nation. The faith that shone brilliantly in the first part of the twelfth chapter of Genesis quickly dissipates as belief and doubt now arm wrestle for control of his mind and behaviour.

Abraham's conduct illuminates a concept most of us are familiar with. It is one thing to excel in faith when all is well; it is another matter altogether to act with triumphant trust when you are literally staring adversity, calamity or death, eyeball to eyeball.

If, as has often been claimed, one's true character rises to the surface when placed in the cauldron of testing, one of the lessons this story from Abraham communicates ought to be a source of significant encouragement to modern readers. You, my friend, are not the first case of dysfunctional faith that God has ever encountered.

I am—beat you to it!

Thankfully, we are usually neither the paragons of spiritual immaturity that we often guilt ourselves into believing we are nor the flawless followers of God we would like others to believe we are. Abraham's behaviour is thus an essential reminder that those who pursue a life of faith will invariably struggle between the selflessness to which we are called as believers and the self-centredness that seems to be so deeply engrained in us as human beings.

As noted earlier, so common today are the moral failings of prominent religious leaders, it can become difficult to refrain from becoming irretrievably cynical concerning the integrity of those who claim to be spiritually devout. For that reason, it is beneficial to pause every now and then and derive refreshing hope from the many impressive examples in church history that spotlight those who did not subscribe to membership in the "it's all about me" club.

One such sterling illustration in this regard was Julian of Norwich, a woman born in fourteenth century England who survived the bubonic plague or Black Death to become a legendary Christian mystic and theologian. Julian contracted the plague in May of 1373 at thirty-one years of age and the last rites were administered shortly thereafter whereupon her mother closed her daughter's eyelids. Julian survived to report that she was transported into heavenly places where she received sixteen visions of a compassionate Christ and words of life and hope to communicate to an illness-wracked community. This she did with unusual power, prompting David Robert Anderson to report:

> Dame Julian was not waiting for a better world in which to rejoice. Bubonic plague and high taxes notwithstanding, she uttered these sublime words: "All shall be well, and all shall be well, and all manner of thing shall be well." (Anderson, 2013, pp. 166–167)

How did Julian of Norwich maintain such an uncommonly triumphant focus in the midst of such trying circumstances? In part, I suggest, because she refused to make allowance in her life for the tempting influences that beckoned in her day with the attractive suggestion to live with the belief that truly "it *is* all about you!"

Fear and doubt wield the power to compromise integrity

Another arresting truth that emerges in the ancient Abraham narrative under consideration has to do with the reality that fear is a fierce deterrent to faith. So too, doubt wields a powerful incentive to compromise integrity.

So far in my life, apart from the time I failed to remember our wedding anniversary, I have never knowingly been confronted with a certain threat that posed an imminent disruption to my longevity. (You might appreciate that the words my beloved shared with me late that summer evening years ago came nowhere near to resembling the endearment one detects in the words of Sarah whom, the Scripture affirms, referred to Abraham her husband as "master" (2 Peter 3:5,6). And, yes, I am confident it likely wasn't during the incident we are looking at in the last half of Genesis 12 that Sarah came up with the designation for Abraham that Peter later claims she once uttered).

At some point in the event we are reviewing from Abraham's life, it evidently strikes him that his physical welfare may be anything but certain. He becomes persuaded the king's attendants may intend to eternally terminate the complications he posed to their plan ("they'll kill me," 12:12). Fearing for his life, he somehow successfully manipulated Sarah into complicity by instructing her to advise these heathen that she was his sister (12:13, 20:14).

And what was the rationale for his attempt to so creatively reconfigure the family tree? Self-preservation: "Say you are my sister, so that I will be treated well and my life will be spared because of you."

What component of your integrity would you or I need very little coaxing to compromise or jettison should the gun be literally pointed at our heads? It may be difficult for most of us to even think in such terms.

Sarah did not seem concerned to even bother arguing with her husband regarding her identity. What was she going to do? Pull out her cell phone and call her brothers or her parents to come and get her? Hop on the next camel back to Canaan or Haran? Truly, her options at this point were decidedly limited.

Apart from the traditional exchange of material assets usually involving livestock and other goods, I have no idea what the marriage vows back in Abraham and Sarah's day looked or sounded like or even if there were such. Having performed numerous marriage ceremonies in parish life over the decades, I have always been interested by the specific terms that modern couples use in choosing what they will say to one another in their wedding vows. I am occasionally surprised by what they select to include or to leave out.

It was once commonplace to hear the groom include a pledge to protect his bride among the other promises made on their wedding day. Such assurances, of course, are the stuff that have bestowed enduring popularity to outstanding novels, dramas and movies that incorporate the imagery of a brave lover risking life and limb to deliver a damsel from distress.

There is no evidence of any such charm at work in this account concerning the calloused attitude Abraham displayed at the prospects of harm coming Sarah's way. Remember, he had the earbuds in listening to *Lookin' Out for #1!* It is both curious and instructive, therefore, that whereas Abraham has been renowned for centuries for his iconic faith in God's promises to make of him a great nation, it is an alarming circumstance that unexpectedly springs up in the course of everyday life that causes his exemplary faith to falter.

Abraham sounds like someone of my acquaintance. I last saw him this morning in the bathroom mirror. Transitioning from winner to loser with respect to the quality of our faith, let us comprehend, can transpire in the blink of an eye. Again, if Abraham's failure was fuelled even in part by the literal hunger that was gnawing in his stomach, it merits our giving due attention to the powerful lure of those devious temptations such as material acquisition, vocational status or plain old fashioned greed or lust, to spur inappropriate behaviour on our part.

When we fail to regularly discipline our minds in more objective times to embed the values and principles that we truly desire to guide our conduct, we are essentially planning for failure. We are leaving allowance for the subjectivity associated with the primal instincts of our humanity to seize the day in moments of weakness. Significant damage to relationships and reputation can quickly ensue with disastrous results that may take a long time to erase from memory and may never be completely repaired.

Regrettably for Abraham on this occasion, unguarded thoughts that were possibly enhanced by hunger led him to act in a manner that compromised his integrity. Sarah's welfare took a backseat to his preoccupation with self-preservation and possibly self-enhancement since he stood to profit handsomely from the transaction (12:16; 13:2). His transition from spiritual winner to spiritual loser was virtually instantaneous. With the speed of lightning his fervent faith was reduced to a feeble flicker.

Grace, forgiveness and restoration are always available for losers who seek such

In trying to beneficially process this troubling incident in the overall context of Abraham's journey of faith, I consider it important to remember that, thankfully, there is always grace, forgiveness, and restoration to be obtained for losers who seek such. As will be seen in the following chapter on Sarah, making this observation is in no way an attempt to mitigate or minimize the negative fallout from Abraham's selfish myopia.

That being said, do not overlook the curious reality that, as far as any kind of immediate consequences for Abraham's actions go, it was the Pharaoh and his household that actually got the raw end of the deal. Go ahead and add that ingredient to your theology of God as loving, just and irreproachable.

Abraham? As noted, he is treated very well by the Pharaoh resulting in a handsome increase to the traveller's net worth. Who says wrongdoing does not pay? By the time Abraham left Egypt the text tells us, he "had become very wealthy in livestock and in silver and gold" (13:2). Not a bad investment, Abe! *Fortune* magazine is on the line wanting an interview. By now his iPod was already playing the next Bachman-Turner Overdrive hit, *Takin' Care of Business* (Bachman-Turner Overdrive, 1973).

As for Pharaoh? Get this, "But the Lord inflicted serious diseases on Pharaoh and his household because of Abraham's wife Sarah" (12:17). What? It is as if God considered the Egyptians completely responsible for what had taken place. So, what is going on with that particular development in this story?

Enns and Byas add insight to this drama in Abraham's life:

> ...Abraham's behaviour leaves something to be desired, which mimics Israel's struggles with God in a nutshell. If you read the story of Abraham's trip to and from Egypt closely, you'll see it clearly mirrors the exodus story. Abraham enters Egypt because of a famine, as would Joseph and the Israelites at the

end of Genesis. Sarah becomes Pharaoh's property, but then he and his household are "plagued" by God for doing so. Pharaoh wants nothing to do with Abraham's God, and summons him to his presence and tells him to leave Egypt, as would another Pharaoh later summon Moses and Aaron and tell the Israelites to leave Egypt. And both Abraham and Israel leave Egypt with a lot of loot. (Enns & Byas, p. 69)

Candidly, if you have never given serious thought to the matter of God's fairness in terms of his dealings with human beings, this would be a good opportunity to lay this book aside for a time and at least attempt to begin processing the workings of the Almighty in this respect. There are many people I have met who have told me in convincing detail that they have essentially come to accept that life is simply not fair, and that God appears to be complicit in a conspiracy against them. Things have not always proven to be as black and white as they were led to believe about God and/or people of faith.

Robert Alter's comments here address what many have found perplexing:

> ...The king is really a good guy. He says, "I have done this with the purity of my hands and the innocence of my heart." And in the Hebrew dialogue, he actually almost stammers. He says something like, "And-and she-she also said that-that she was his sister." When Abraham talks, at first he has no answer for Abimelech. He talks in a kind of lawyerly circumlocution, saying, "Well, in fact, she is, after all, from a certain point of view, my sister, because she's my half-sister" and so forth. So the father of Israel looks not so good, and the other turns out to be the moral exemplar." (Moyers, (Ed.), p. 168)

Against this slightly disturbing backdrop, then, we are eventually informed in Genesis 13 that Abraham retrieves Sarah and engages in some backtracking toward the Negev where he had previously built an altar and called on the name of the Lord (12:8). Upon his return to Bethel after the Pharaoh could not act fast enough in telling him to "git," the text simply states that Abraham again called on the name of the Lord.

At this point in our musings on this incident, the reader of Scripture has some challenging decisions to make as to how little or how much to make of Abraham's calling on the name of the Lord (13:4). To approach the issue from another angle, as St. Paul once instructed his aspiring student preacher, Timothy, in 2 Timothy 2:15, how should we go about "accurately handling the word of truth" at this point?

In this quest, I cannot help but remember the wisdom contained in the frequent warnings of one of my seminary professors, Old Testament scholar Dr. Walter C. Kaiser, Jr., whose work I have already cited. Dr. Kaiser repeatedly cautioned us as aspiring pastors that what can often be "good for the blessing" when preaching can simultaneously "be bad for the text" in terms of responsible interpretation. His insistent plea to "keep our finger on the text" was his unique means of beseeching us to beware of the dangers of "reading into" the text by "introducing something into the narrative that simply is not there" in the interests of building a homiletically attractive argument. (I will be forever grateful for Dr. Kaiser's ever humorous contributions in spurring us to careful conscientiousness in handling the Old Testament text. Accordingly, perhaps I should also beg his indulgence for my interpretation here of 13:4's "there Abram called on the name of the Lord").

I, therefore, proceed somewhat cautiously to register a truth which, after prolonged reflection, I trust can be legitimately supported by, if not this specific text, then via the overall testimony of Scripture. ("Forgive me, Dr. Kaiser, for perhaps I have sinned")?

Although the text under scrutiny here does not explicitly say so, I submit that it is reasonable to assume that Abraham's act of devotion at Bethel (Hebrew for "house of God") prompted some serious soul searching on his part as he reflected on what had recently transpired in the incident involving Sarah and the Pharaoh in Egypt. Could this time of devotion for Abraham have prompted him to confess his self-centred ways that led to his directing Sarah to lie regarding her identity? Might the time at Bethel have become a period of reconciliation between Abraham and God? I humbly advance that asking such questions points to the distinct possibility that Abraham faced his failure at this juncture.

On a more domestic note, perhaps this back to Bethel incident also included a time of answering a few questions from Sarah in the course of engaging in some necessary marital repair. Thus, Abraham made some amends with both God and Sarah.

I think it is entirely possible that Abraham's reflection at Bethel involved an appeal to God for restoration leading to a fresh encounter of the Lord's cleansing and renewing grace. I will let you decide for yourself concerning these relevant matters, but I judge that it is not unreasonable to conclude that something of personal spiritual significance may well have occurred for Abraham in returning to Bethel.

What does appear obvious is that from the perspective of what is widely considered to be Christian behaviour or a Christian ethic in twenty-first century North America, it is legitimate to assert that Abraham's behaviour in Egypt was less than exemplary for a man historically renowned for his great faith. We often speak of our similar personal failures in terms of "blowing it," "letting a loved one down" or "failing God." This is a story wherein Abraham appears to have blown it in a big way.

Regardless of the terms we may assign to Abraham's or our own shortcomings, the relevant lesson here is the realization that the same grace that enabled Abraham to re-engage the blessing of God following his failure in Egypt is available to modern people of faith when we stumble from the path of devout faith.

Despite how we may choose to interpret the critical and textual issues related to the account in chapter 20 of Genesis regarding a similar case of poor conduct by Abraham, we also need to consider

God is Loser Friendly

the contents of Genesis 26 where it seems Isaac seems to have picked up on a few of his Dad's bad habits. Abraham, man of great faith that he was, struggled on occasion with honesty.

I can relate. Can you?

It is apparent that the writer(s) of Genesis saw this behavioural penchant in this family as a matter worthy of repetition for their authorial purposes. It thus warrants the question: why is this behaviour documented three times in early Genesis? What are we intended to glean from such a reality regarding this legendary hero of the faith?

Interesting and instructive as such matters may be, be sure not to miss the implicit message ultimately offered by this emphasis on Abraham & Sons' struggle with misrepresenting the facts when such was expedient: famous recipients of God's grace are often very adept at demonstrating their ongoing need of an even greater measure of his grace. A fall from grace always seems more traumatic for all concerned when the one who falls has a prominent profile. We therefore ought not to minimize Abraham's tumble.

Following the very public debacle back in the late 1980s that proved to be the end of Jim and Tammy Bakker's PTL television empire, I made time to read Bakker's subsequent book titled *I Was Wrong*. Regardless of whether or not we will ever truly know exactly what transpired in that surreal fiasco or to what extent Bakker truly owned up to the truth, I think it is helpful to try and view such travesties and those that I referred to at the start of Chapter Two through the lens of the three directives I have isolated from this story of Abraham. I have attempted to find the proper balance between reading too much into the story and entirely missing the point of the anecdote(s) from an authorial perspective.

God's people occasionally do stupid things. Indeed, God's people on occasion do sinful things—to the extent that at times our behaviour is minimally different from those who make no claim at all to be religious or Christian. Further, at times, God appears to offer absolutely nothing by way of a rebuke or an attempt to correct the guilty party. Thus it has ever been, apparently.

Nonetheless, you and I are not God and are therefore not entitled to pronounce final explanation, rationalization or judgment when we learn of people of faith who have conducted themselves inappropriately. Our energies are better spent on resisting the temptation to respond with dogmatic criticism. It is preferable to cultivate a mindset that responds to news of a fall from grace by looking for a concrete opportunity to extend grace to someone we know who needs it. It may be a loved one; it may be a stranger. Just do it!

The God of Abraham, it appears, is very practised at extending grace to spiritual losers. He has a lengthy record of returning people from the Loser roll to the Honour roll because God is loser friendly. And that is truly good news for believers who are lamenting their own personal failures. For what it means is that we too will find God waiting to extend his undeserving favour to us whenever we get around to returning to our Bethel.

Toward such a realization, helpful insights from Lewis Smedes and Eugene Rivers III, participants on the Moyers panel, serve as an appropriate conclusion to our visit with father Abraham:

> For us Christians, Abraham is our father, not because he's a good guy, but because he is the reminder that our relationship with the Almighty is a relationship defined by grace. What really matters is not whether Abraham is good or bad or cowardly or heroic, but that God pursues His design for the welfare of the human family with people like that—in other words, people like us ... [Abraham's] faith is a model to me because if I want to know whether I am at peace with my Maker, the answer has to be found in the grace of the Maker, not in the quality of the person. (Moyers, (Ed.), pp. 170–171)

I resonate with Abraham, and I identify with his frailty and humanity. I love the fact that from this story I know that an eternal God will be in conversation with the most broken, mischievous, pragmatic, and self-centered individual. Then, on other occasions, that same individual, inspired by God, can be elevated to heights of heroism. (Ibid., p. 183)

Chapter Four:
When God Has the Last Laugh
(Genesis 16–18, 21)

*One secret of life is that the reason life works at all
is that not everyone in your tribe is nuts on the same day.
Another secret is that laughter is carbonated holiness.*
(Anne Lamott, 2005, pp. 65–66)

Several years before they passed on, my parents gave each of their five children a pictorial booklet they had compiled that summarized their personal histories. The project covered their childhoods as well as details surrounding how they had met, fallen in love and coped throughout the early years of their marriage while separated by Dad's enlistment in the Canadian Army during World War II.

Upon reviewing their efforts, I phoned Dad and Mom to register a minor complaint. "I note the volume contains no anecdotes at all regarding some of the arguments and disagreements I recall you having over sixty plus years of marriage," I protested. "Nor do I find any evidence of the uncivil wars the five ingrates you raised used to wage on a consistent basis. This is a rather sanitized version of life in our home as I recall it," I needled them further. "In fact, it serves as a sterling example of what academics call historical revisionism."

Most of us prefer not to acknowledge, recall or otherwise document our failings, shortcomings and imperfections. We would rather people merely speculate concerning that kind of information about us in the course of realizing what everyone in due course recognizes about themselves: at times we all can be real losers. We snarl at the kids, kick the cat, and yell at our partner. We prefer others not be aware that on occasion, many occasions in fact, we are inclined to lie, lust, loathe and leer.

We would rather others think of us the way many of us appeared at church on Sunday morning when we were children—fresh from a Saturday night bath, with clean clothing, combed hair, a smile in place, memory verses learned and a Gideons New Testament with The Psalms in hand. Remember how we were presented as creatures of decorum with all of our character blemishes temporarily hidden from view thanks to a dab or two of saintly cosmetics?

Reading the book of Genesis can be a bit of a shock given that, when it comes to reviewing the history of the people of faith, the Bible is neither cosmetically nor politically correct. In the opening pages of the *Torah* we find an abundance of the kind of lying, cheating, scheming and immorality generally featured via modern media outlets such as the *National Enquirer* or TMZ.com. Reading Genesis at times can be like watching an episode of the once popular, if unruly, Jerry Springer television show.

If you are reading this book as a professing Christ follower but have never yet felt like a spiritual loser, that is directly related to the unavoidable fact that you are physically dead. Sorry to be the dispenser of troubling news, but as a believer who knows my own heart and has served as a pastor in several churches over more than three decades, I owe you the uncomfortable truth. If you are breathing, you are guilty of a similar waywardness to what we have already noted in the life of Abraham and will now observe in the experience of his wife, Sarah.

Sarah's frame of mind after the Pharaoh incident

Let's listen in again to the PBS panel discussion and hear Bill Moyers question Bharati Mukjerkee:

> But what do you make of Sarah's silence? I find Abraham's behaviour more understandable than Sarah's. Either she's playing along with the decep-

> tion willingly or she feels she has to do it. She's cast into Pharaoh's harem. She's passed off as something she isn't. Her husband is hiding behind her skirts. And yet, in this brief account, we have no indication what is going through her mind. (Moyers, (Ed.), p. 165)
>
> I think Sarah is actually exercising power in other ways—she's consolidating her superiority over Abraham. She's been humiliated. Now she can say, "You owe me one. When we get out of this situation, I'm going to cash in the chips." (Ibid., p. 165)

We are given no immediate indication as to the relational fallout that Abraham's attempt to trick the Pharaoh likely produced between Abraham and Sarah. In fact, from what is communicated in the remainder of Genesis 12, we might assume that perhaps Sarah had gone along with her husband's plan for reasons that are not made clear.

Think about that with me for a few moments. Did Sarah really have much of a choice? In all probability there was no women's shelter nearby to grant her safe haven from an abusive husband. No women's HELP-line to call. No ladies' Bible study to summon for prayer and emotional support.

What *is* evident is that, reflecting the patriarchal culture of the time, Pharaoh holds Abraham responsible when ill health arrived in the former's community shortly after Sarah moved in. Upon the Lord's infliction of serious diseases on Pharaoh's household, Pharaoh scurries about and learns Sarah's true identity. He then summons Abraham and demands that he give account for his deceit.

Notice again that the initial consequences of Abraham's attempted manipulation of Pharaoh do not fall on Abraham. The Egyptians were the ones running to the bathroom in the middle of the night! This is a most interesting dynamic that will surface again in the narrative of Genesis as people of faith seem to consistently avoid incurring any immediate penalty for their wrongdoing. God, it strikes me, cannot be bothered to issue so much as even a stern reprimand or a rap on the knuckles to Abraham for his inappropriate, indeed, unethical conduct. All we are told along this line has to do with God's reaffirmation of blessing to Abraham in chapter 15.

As if this observation alone is not enough to trouble conscientious readers, note also that the author(s) of Genesis do(es) not clarify whether Abraham was required to return the ample amount of livestock he had acquired in the initial business transaction effected with Pharaoh regarding his "sister." Abraham seemed to be quite enjoying the lucrative profits of his questionable behaviour without any apparent confrontation from God for his blatant dishonesty in deceiving Pharaoh. We are thus left to speculate regarding Sarah's overall psychological welfare, or any negative ramifications incurred for Abraham and Sarah's relationship as a result of the Pharaoh incident. Being the modern readers that we are, the absence of anything reminiscent of one of those "honey, we need to talk" conversation starters comes across as curious.

Perhaps we are merely witnessing the frank realities of a patriarchal culture where women were regarded as "chattel" or possessions and were expected to simply take what their husbands dished out. Whatever the explanation for this aspect of the story, several modern North American women who have listened to me preach on this incident have not hesitated at all to offer a few choice observations to me afterward regarding their perspectives on that dimension of ancient domestic life.

Karen Armstrong grants today's readers some useful contextualization as to how we ought to think about the behaviour of the ancients in this regard:

> ... [T]he patriarchs were not family men. Whatever their other achievements, their domestic lives left much to be desired. They were frequently highly unsatisfactory as husbands and disastrous as parents. Blessing should radiate from a man who has received the divine favour to those around him, and

the first people to benefit should be his immediate family. The fact that all three of the patriarchs signally failed in this is just one more indication of the difficulty of living successfully and compassionately in the divine presence." (Armstrong, p. 62)

Three additional chapters of Genesis (13–15) are devoted to God's continued blessing of Abraham following the Pharaoh-Sarah fiasco before any attention whatsoever is given to Sarah's emotional state or the deteriorating condition of her faith. When the reader's attention is finally directed to Sarah in chapter 16, it is not surprising at all to find her deeply agitated.

What's to be learned from Sarah's schooling in faith?

Burton L. Visotzky underscores well the pent-up emotions that eventually got the best of Sarah:

> When Abraham gives Sarah over to Pharaoh back in Egypt, she doesn't say a word. Now [chapter 16] she gets ferocious and immediately turns to physical abuse. The Hebrew term used for her abuse of Hagar is exactly the same term used later in the Book of Exodus when the Egyptians abuse the Hebrew slaves." (Moyers, (Ed.), p. 191)

Despite the understandable acrimony that lingers in the background as Sarah moves into the spotlight in the sections of Genesis we are now considering, I wish to call attention to three primary insights that emerge from the narrative which I suggest offer twenty-first century readers ample food for thought.

Firstly, Sarah's behaviour in Genesis 16 points to the reality that life's inequities can make faith seem futile, if not downright foolish. Do not overlook the reality that this woman's anger is initially directed at the Lord. She is certain that her inability to conceive is God's fault; he has kept her from having children.

It is not at all uncommon for someone to come to me as their pastor and confide something along the line of, "Pastor, I am angry at God because of this or that which is or isn't happening in my life." I learned long ago that the most realistic response I can offer such inquirers begins with something like, "You are going to have to take a number, because there are quite a few people ahead of you in that line-up." So many people are hesitant to admit having anger at God that sometimes in the interests of saving time I will cut to the chase and say, "I think what you are trying to tell me is that you are upset with God. Please don't feel bad. There is no better time to admit it than now since it is not like he is in the dark on the matter, is it?"

Beginning with a Scripture similar to Sarah's behaviour here, I commence to point out that God's apparent lack of concern or care-less-ness has been a feature of the divine-human relationship right from the beginning. That does not mean we have to necessarily like the fact because, lest we forget, God is not surfing Facebook waiting for us to indicate our "like" for what he or she is or isn't posting in our lives. But it is advantageous to recognize that thoughts and feelings along this line are an inevitable component of the faith journey and that men and women more devout than we have found themselves at similar places in life. And, yes, sometimes more than once. Ultimately, there is nothing to be gained by denying or dismissing anger at God. Experiencing such is merely par for the course.

Concerning Sarah's frame of mind here, Bruce Feiler writes:

> ...Sarah takes her maid and gives her to Abraham in an echo of the way Eve takes the fruit and gives it to Adam. Again the implication is unavoidable: Sarah is trying to wrest control of creation, which Abraham and God are already struggling over. **Abraham may be wavering in his faith, but Sarah seems to have abandoned hers.** Her act may be selfless, but it's also faithless." (Feiler, 2002, p. 64) (emphasis added)

Sarah's frustrated and possibly failing faith leads her to conclude that God could obviously use some help in fulfilling the promise he had made to Abraham and, implicitly, to herself. So, she directs Abraham to sleep with her servant, Hagar. Enns and Byas help reduce the shock that modern readers may experience here when they point out: "...remember that God didn't mention Sarah in his promise to Abraham, he never said who the mother would be. Also, this type of surrogate mother to ensure descendants is a known practice of the ancient world" (Enns & Byas, p. 71).

Abraham, giant of the faith that he is, apparently needs no convincing to comply with Sarah's directive. He does not even appear to suggest they might first consider visiting a marriage counsellor or get an appointment at an infertility clinic. He is equally anxious to get this show on the road. Thus, on the sole basis of Sarah's encouragement, Abraham obliges and sleeps with Hagar.

A lifelong friend who has spent a considerable portion of his career involved dispensing humanitarian aid to third world countries recently reminded me that the pressures on an infertile woman in many societies, including our own, are not to be underestimated. In some of the cultures in which he has worked, infertile women are given designations that indicate to all the fact of their infertility. Some locales do not allow infertile females to have conversation or social interaction with other women, particularly pregnant ones, or permit them to have any contact whatsoever with newborns. In places that sanction a man taking more than one wife, the shame of the second wife becoming pregnant before the first wife can be overwhelming and very few people would actually believe that the first wife consented to such a development.

When Hagar reports that she is pregnant, therefore, Sarah's meltdown is apparently not surprising or exceptional given cultural standards that still exist in parts of our modern world. Redirecting her compounding anger toward the expectant mother, accordingly, may have been primarily due to her realization that everyone would conclude that she, not Abraham, was evidently responsible for their inability to achieve pregnancy as a couple. A whirlwind of potential realities and strong emotions may well be at play in Sarah's circumstances. All manner of questions are therefore legitimate for inquisitive modern readers who are several millennia removed from the cultures on display in Genesis.

Relational complications arising from such troubling realities have often come up when I have been called on to address fertility issues with couples. One layer of disappointment, blame, shame or guilt ends up getting buried beneath another and then another as time goes by. When it is fuelled by anger or shame at oneself, at a partner or at God, it can become a very explosive matter with immense implications for a couple's individual and collective faith.

Due to whatever is going on emotionally and spiritually in this story, Sarah eventually explodes at Abraham for the humiliation and angst she is feeling. "*You* are responsible for the wrong I am suffering...." (16:5). I can well imagine Abraham defensively reminding Sarah as to just who it was that had introduced Hagar into the equation.

Sarah's angst simmers and periodically boils over. Eventually, she so mistreats Hagar that the Egyptian mother can take no more, "Enough of this. I'm outta here!"

Ouch! A catfight and a marital spat just a few verses after God has confirmed to Abraham that all will be well. Sarah's tank of faith is nudging the empty mark and the questions have to be piling up in Abraham's mind also.

To be kind to Sarah, let us not overlook that so far on this perplexing sojourn with Abraham, she has not experienced much fairness. The text, for example, gives us no indication that she had been party to Abraham's original call from God. This factor prompts Lewis Smedes to insightfully surmise: "what if Abraham were the only one to hear the call? Somebody else might have said, "You think God came to you in a dream. I think you just dreamed that God came to you." There's a big difference" (Moyers, (Ed.), p. 159).

My pastoral experience has shown me that Sarah was not the last woman to experience the frustration of establishing her role in a scenario where she had some legitimate grounds for questioning whether her husband truly knew what he was doing. I recall a couple in one church I served telling me they were considering yet another move, their fourth in five years, owing to his vocation. As we chatted about their situation, I noticed the wife roll her eyes in frustration as she commented somewhat emphatically: "it seems like we're barely settled in one place before he's off again! I'm so tired of this game."

Perhaps Sarah could relate. The focus of the Abraham and Sarah story so far has been on how God is leading Abraham to leave his homeland and travel in stages toward a new home yet to be confirmed. Initially, Sarah is portrayed as a background figure, the loving and supportive wife content to go along with hubby's plan. She deserves full credit for attempting to deal with the disruption brought into her life by a major relocation, a famine and a war in addition to the animosity and conflict that existed between Abraham and his nephew, Lot.

And do not forget, there had also been that uncomfortable matter of having to endure a manipulative husband who coerced her into lying and to likely compromise her morals in an effort to spare his own skin. Her personal welfare in the midst of traumatic domestic upheaval does not seem to have even registered with Abraham who was hardly living with his wife in a "considerate" or "understanding" manner. (For some reason, when I read the commendation of Sarah as an exemplary wife in the 1 Peter 3:5–7 passage to which I referred earlier, I again find myself wondering what Sarah might have had to say by way of response to Peter had she had the opportunity).

Sarah's faith is faltering. It seems it is always Abraham getting the affirmations from God that things are going to turn out all right, that they will have a son and become a great nation, and so forth. Genesis 15 informs us that when Abraham complains to God out of his own frustration and questions what good all these promises and blessings were when he still did not have a son. God responds with a vision indicating Abraham merely needs to persevere and all will be well.

Was Sarah a part of those interactions between God and her husband? Did her husband share with her about his own frustrations and doubts and how God was resolving them and reassuring him? Did he give Sarah an opportunity to vent her frustrations on the matter? Or, as we men are known to do, did he keep all of those matters to himself and expect his wife to simply trust his wisdom since, after all, "I am the head of the home, honey?"

Possibly, Abraham was like many husbands in terms of his lack of communication skills and the accompanying inclination to retreat into his man-cave with minimal indication to the Mrs. as to what was really going on in his head and heart. Abraham may have been unaware of it, but he is definitely contributing to Sarah's faith becoming futile.

Not surprisingly then, Sarah is in her own full-fledged crisis of faith. She had heard the talk about this great nation she was supposed to be part of. Yet as month after month went by with no indication that she was pregnant, she can hardly be blamed for crying out to God, "Hello, up there, it's me. I'm not getting any younger, you know! Have I done something wrong to turn you against me?"

God bless her candor.

How do you respond when you conclude God has forgotten about you or maybe even given up on you? Do you think of cashing it all in and just becoming a cantankerous sceptic? Do you blame yourself? Conclude it is something you have done or have not done? Try and undo what you did that you now think maybe you should not have done?

But nothing changes.

Sooner or later you become convinced you are left with only one conclusion: life is not fair and, come to think of it, neither is God. You start questioning the value of faith and looking for another option to, at minimum, try and save face for God. You inwardly wince when anyone inquires as to how you are doing and if everything is okay.

Say what we might about Sarah's plan born of frustration, it brings to mind another wife in the Bible whose frank counsel to a husband's plans gone awry tendered an even a more drastic solution. "Are you still holding on to your integrity? Curse God and die," Job's wife candidly advised her husband in the midst of his trying to come to terms with the devastation life had dealt him (Job 1, 2).

Amidst the periodic tempests that are encountered in trying to lead a life of faith, I urge you to learn to be gentle with yourself. Accept that life's inequities will sometimes make faith look futile, if not downright laughable or foolish, and that your experience in that regard is not at all unusual in the expedition of faith.

A second instructive offered in the Sarah story that I have already briefly acknowledged bids us to be ever mindful that life's inequities may tempt us to take matters into our own hands.

Sarah's first major role in the Genesis account has a rather bleak back story. She emerges from the Pharaoh anecdote as a mistreated and perhaps even an abused woman. Some modern readers have suggested to me they see elements of emotional abuse or even domestic violence at play in 12:10–20.

Several insecurities are stalking Sarah. She has been on an emotional roller-coaster in the matter of lying to Pharaoh. Abraham appears to be a less than sensitive husband in several regards. She is advancing in age while listening to him confidently relay God's insistence they would indeed have children of their own. So, it is hardly surprising to encounter Sarah in a funk when the spotlight finally shines on her (16:2).

Having come to believe that God is not fair and with the promise of her having her own son looking more like a mirage with each passing month, Sarah decides to kick her own plan into action. It is a strategy that certainly would not earn the endorsement today of the American Religious Right or organizations like Focus on the

Family, but the course of conduct she selected was not unusual in the local customs of her day.

Like most women, Sarah is no dummy. She had possibly been formulating Option B for some time already with optimism that she might somehow keep her husband from completely embarrassing them both. After all, like most men, Abraham would probably have been boasting to his pals about God's call and promise to make of him a great nation. There was one seemingly insurmountable problem, however. Nothing was happening on the fertility front for Abraham and Sarah.

"Hey Abraham," she slyly poses, "remember a while ago when you were fearing for your life and let me be taken into Pharaoh's harem in order to save your own neck? Well, guess what, my dear? You owe me one! So here is the plan: Hagar is going to help us out with this family thing."

Abraham, being male, or for whatever combination of reasons related to his own frustrations with what God was promising but not producing, needed very little encouragement to go along with Sarah's plan. Crises of faith can serve as an irresistible lure to come up with some creative notions. And somebody else's crisis of faith, especially that of a loved one, may produce an atmosphere for temptation to take root when we are desperate to see their faith strengthened.

Why not? Solving your own problems or helping others solve theirs is a popular strategy today. Scores of twenty-first century rationalists would say it is the only sensible and responsible way forward. All you have to do is listen to some of the vacuities being aired on religious radio and TV programs today to understand why many people do not hesitate to articulate their disdain for those who piously cling to religious faith instead of using their own smarts to resolve the inequities of life.

In his discerning book, *The Sibling Society*, Robert Bly capably summarizes that we live in a society which encourages participants to take our primary cues for how to live from what we pick up in our horizontal relationships (Bly, 1997). Numerous voices today advise us to jettison outdated tales about a vertical relationship with God or some notion of a Higher Power. If we are not looking out for ourselves and our own best interests, we are told, we truly are losers who deserve all of the complications and frustrations that life invariably sends our way.

Given such ever present influences, the temptation to bail God out or to give him some help and do it all myself can become a most uncomfortable place for a believer to find herself. What is your inclination when solving your problems with your own common sense seems like the best thing to do if for no other reason than that it appears God may very well embarrass himself by having promised something he cannot deliver?

It is at this juncture that the balance of Sarah's story in Genesis issues a flashing, amber caution light. Be sure not to overlook that, tempting as it is to give in to the voices of popular culture, taking matters into our own hands runs the risk of compounding our problems.

Sarah's backup plan almost immediately encounters several awkward complications. Upon becoming pregnant, Hagar turns vindictive toward Sarah and begins to taunt her for the latter's inability to conceive. Matters related to maternal health are complex and have been known to bring out both the best and the worst in women. It is not uncommon for the emotional stability of an expectant mother to be eroded.

At the time of writing, I am attempting to give pastoral support to three young couples all wrestling with various difficulties related to the issue of (in)fertility. Such is part of the reason I maintain that the days when women stoically lost pregnancies and shared it with no one but their husbands rightfully belong in the past. Whenever I hear people pine for the good old days of domestic practices or family life, I remind them that those good old days included the appalling routine where men often went to work or to play golf while their wives gave birth. "Are those the good old days you wish to retrieve?" I will skeptically inquire.

One of the couples I am supporting has already lost several pregnancies to miscarriages; another spent a small fortune trying to get pregnant via the best medical methodologies and counsel available to young couples in the twenty-first century before pregnancy finally occurred; the other couple, who lost a little one at 38 weeks a couple of years ago just recently and joyfully welcomed a healthy baby boy into their home.

These couples have all been diligently attempting to bolster one another through uncertain and anxious times. I am privileged they have permitted me to learn along with them. We have discovered that acquiring the skills to truly rejoice with those who rejoice and weep with those who weep is far easier said than done when it comes to such personal and intimate concerns. Attempting to cope when God seems far away and unconcerned is much easier to do when you face life's challenges in tandem with supportive friends given that matters related to (in)fertility can elicit the most visceral of emotions and reactions.

In the fallout from attempting to resolve her infertility issues in her own way, Sarah's emotions are all over the map. She turns on Abraham warning him that God will make him pay for what *she* told him to do. In 16:6, she vindictively kicks Hagar out on the street and is not satisfied until, as chapter 21 informs us, she succeeds in having Hagar and her newborn son completely run out of town. Can you imagine the tongues that started wagging in Abraham and Sarah's community as that scenario played out?

Sarah's experiment reminds us that, during those times when living by faith seems futile, the flipside of that coin is that succumbing to the enticing inclination to function on auto pilot and go solely with your own solutions may create even more problems or introduce bigger questions and complications than those that initially confronted us.

Chapter Four: When God Has the Last Laugh

Living in a culture that often belittles faith in God by advising us to be masters of our own fate, it is understandable that attempting to supply our own answers to the challenges of life is seen as a tempting and viable option. It runs the risk, however, of doing little more than compounding our problems. Be careful not to miss Sarah's flashing, amber caution light or her road sign that directs us to Proceed With Caution, lest the potential complications we introduce to our existing bewilderment prove to be overwhelming.

Fortunately, compounding our problems by taking matters into our own hands does not necessarily have to be the last chapter in anyone's story. God is gracious enough to regain operational control of the disaster we are either courting or have already set in motion.

As a result of Sarah's experience, a third instructive consideration in this narrative is that it should buttress our faith to note that God's grace shines through even when taking matters into our own hands turns out to truly bungle things. Out of an account wherein human manipulation, blame and vindictiveness are prominently profiled, God's plan retains the upper hand and his faithfulness ultimately prevails. And Sarah is not thrown on the scrap heap of life for her faithless manipulation in trying to do God's work for him.

Not in the least.

Genesis 21:1, 2 states, "Now the Lord was gracious to Sarah as he had said, and the Lord did for Sarah what he had promised. Sarah became pregnant and bore a son to Abraham in his old age." There is that notion of undeserving favour again. God's original plan does not falter.

Despite Sarah's compulsive strategizing to rescue God from embarrassing himself, Isaac is eventually born to this elderly couple. God keeps his promise thereby reminding us that God's plans are not thwarted by the dysfunctional inclinations of the human instruments necessary to effect the fulfilment of his plans.

There is a sense, of course, in which Sarah's basic problem was that she found it difficult if not impossible to wait for God's promise to see the light of day. If such was difficult for her to do in an era when God apparently spoke audibly to people and was known, on occasion, to have his emissaries drop by for lunch, should it surprise us as contemporary believers that we often find it frustrating to wait for God to come through in our lives?

I detest waiting. Participating in a society that features ever higher speeds by which to download internet data, coffee machines that dispense fresh brew in seconds and credit card payments accommodated by merely tapping the card against another handheld plastic device, it is not difficult to discern why I am annoyed by having to wait.

As a kid growing up on the frigid prairies of western Canada, many of my Saturday afternoons were spent at the ice-skating arena. Located in the ample foyer of that facility was a vending machine that allegedly dispensed cans of soda pop. We could secure a Coke for a dime! (I know; like Abraham, I am ancient. My offspring frequently remind me of the reality).

That vending machine was the source of much frustration and many life lessons. It would frequently steal our dimes without dispensing anything. Or we would hear the can begin to roll down the chute somewhere within the contraption only to have the refreshment get stuck and leave us thirstier and crankier. We would holler at the machine. We would kick it. We even tried rocking it back and forth in our quest to dislodge the product we had ordered and paid for. We would vocally and physically abuse that inanimate vendor until, eventually, dear Mrs. Van Biezen would bellow at us to "leave dat machine alone!" and wander over from the confection counter with the key.

After endless statements and queries suggesting she sincerely doubted the veracity of our grievances, she would eventually extract our can of soda all the while airing additional scepticisms concerning our honesty. Of all the nerve!

Chapter Four: When God Has the Last Laugh

The truth is that despite having an earned doctorate in religious history, I still have not mastered how to stop occasionally treating God like that old vending-machine in my hometown arena: 1) identify desired product or solution; 2) push button or submit obligatory prayer; 3) await immediate action from machine or God. If such is not immediately forthcoming, bellow at God, kick him if nobody is looking, vent to anybody who will listen ... and so forth. (I first encountered the notion of God being treated as a vending machine in the insightful book *God is Not a Vending Machine* (Hinten, 1983).

I am more like Sarah than I care to admit. So are you.

Abraham and Sarah name their miracle baby, "he laughs," as an enduring testimony to the truth that God usually has the last laugh when it comes to resolving the entanglements of the predicaments that we of weak faith can inhabit. Isaac would serve as an ongoing reminder to his aged parents that, at its core, faith is about holding on to God's promise even when you know people are rolling their eyes, shaking their heads and engaging their tongues behind your back. In the middle of the night when they would get up to care for him, Isaac was a wailing indicator that God is known to be trustworthy even when friends are advising you not to be foolish, stupid or to "get in touch with reality, already!"

And I am sure they smiled, just as I am learning to smile every time I am confronted with the frailty of my faith. That means I am frequently smiling.

The story of Sarah in Genesis is that God's grace is more than capable of picking up the pieces of the messes we excel at creating and complicating. Perhaps today you find yourself in the middle of one of those complex stretches of life that has become so convoluted you cannot even remember how it got to be so messy.

Sarah knew what it was to be at such a point. She knew how tempting it was to look in the mirror and, using her thumb and index finger, affix a capital L to her forehead.

Meanwhile, God never lost sight of his promise regarding the certainty of that day when Sarah was able to declare: "God has brought me laughter, and everyone who hears about this will laugh with me" (21:6).

The compelling lesson from her life is that God may also be looking to have the last laugh in your life. And mine.

Chapter Five:
The Mess at Sodom
(Genesis 18–19)

*I know the world is loved by God, as are all of its people,
but it is much easier to believe that God hates or disapproves
of or punishes the same people I do, because these thoughts are
what is going on inside me much of the time.*
(Anne Lamott, 2005, pp. 220–221)

Have you ever noticed how merely hearing the name of a certain location in the world can bring sinister images and unpleasant associations to mind?

For those in today's older age groups, this happens when places like Auschwitz or Ravensbrück are mentioned. These infamous sites still summon deep grief and intense anger for scores of people around the world who lost loved ones in the German concentration camps established in Eastern Europe during World War II. Pearl Harbour, Hiroshima, Nagasaki are ominous regions that are among some of the tragic names from the same era.

How about Jonestown? Jim Jones, an American cult leader stunned civilization and earned notoriety in November 1978 when he convinced hundreds of his followers in what was called The Peoples Temple to commit mass suicide in the country of Guyana in northern South America.

Waco, Texas. My generation will never forget being riveted to television screens back in 1993 as a fateful standoff involving David Koresh and the Branch Davidians captured the world's attention and secured that city a place of infamy in history books. The six-episode drama *Waco* was recently released to one of the TV movie super-networks educating an entirely new generation to the frightening events of those days of yesteryear.

Lac Magantic, Quebec. Forty-five people died and the core of a quaint French-Canadian village gutted in July 2013 when the brakes failed on a freight train parked on an incline not far from that town. Railcars loaded with crude oil rolled backwards into the village where they derailed creating a devastating fireball.

The modern era of international terrorism has visited more disrepute upon numerous other major centres over the past thirty years or so: Nairobi, Lower Manhattan, Bali, London, Paris, Nice. Many, if not most of us, live with a quiet fear that "it could happen here."

America's absurd infatuation with guns is such that place names like Columbine, Sandy Hook, Orlando, Baton Rouge, Pittsburgh and El Paso have been forever stained with the blood of innocent victims guilty of nothing but shopping or attending school, a concert or worship.

And then there is Sodom and Gomorrah, a couple of ancient cities that to this day continue to evoke images and thoughts of perversion and judgment whenever they are mentioned. Many of us grew up hearing the story of Sodom and Gomorrah interpreted through the lens of how much God hates sin and how utterly devastating his judgment on iniquity can be. It remains popular today in some circles for Christian preachers to still use this ancient story to denounce the evils of what is often referred to as "the homosexual agenda."

If we give careful attention to this story in Genesis, however, there is much here to substantiate the claim that God is gracious, that catastrophic judgement is never his initial preference. That's right. Even within the foreboding account of Sodom and Gomorrah, there are distinct elements indicating that God is indeed loser friendly.

God is relentless in his pursuit of losers

It may prove helpful to readers to be reminded that my purpose in reviewing these accounts in Genesis does not include expending excessive energy puzzling over whether or not God approves of the kind of illicit behaviour we encounter in the text. Bear in mind, as I mentioned earlier, that there is much to be gained by making the effort to read these stories in the same manner as we read any book. That is, to remember that we are not usually aware of information that lies ahead in portions yet to be read.

Accordingly, it is not possible for what we have not yet read to inform or influence what we are currently reading. I maintain that it is worthwhile to simply read these stories as they are presented without immediately interpreting them in light of The Ten Commandments or other aspects of a moral code to be encountered later in the Bible.

To register this point from a different angle, perhaps it is helpful to point out that the writer(s) of Genesis at times seem(s) to have minimal interest in anything that looks or sounds like a divine denunciation of unrighteous behaviour. It is advantageous for us as readers, therefore, to not become unnecessarily absorbed with that pursuit particularly as it relates to this story.

An honest attempt in this regard lends credibility to the suggestion that a major theme derived from these graphic accounts is that God's affection for his beloved is far, far greater than his dismay over their ill-advised blunders. It bears repeating that wrongdoing in Genesis is often portrayed with minimal emphasis given to anything other than the stark facts.

The silence of the first book of the Bible in this respect implicitly conveys the message that the spotlight in the drama is not focused on man's wickedness. Instead, it shines on the astounding truth that it is not only difficult but, in fact, it is actually impossible for those whom God so passionately loves to shake his persistent affection. We may stumble and fall many times in our walk of faith, and we all do, but that in no way changes the reality that God is stubbornly loser friendly.

This dynamic is richly underscored in the story of Sodom and Gomorrah, an account which some have erroneously concluded does not contain much of a positive nature. I disagree with that assessment which leads me to advance a couple of positive directives from the scandalous story of that mess at Sodom.

The people of a loser friendly God should be loser friendly as well.

A concept that people of faith do well to periodically contemplate relates to what others are likely to conclude about the nature of God by observing our lives, demeanours and attitudes. Another way of approaching the matter is to advocate for occasionally pondering what kind of a public relations job we are doing as those who claim to know and love the compassionate God portrayed in Scripture.

It may be useful for you to again pause in your reading at this point and take a few moments to candidly review your day or your week from this perspective. Be honest with yourself and with God. You may find it helpful to include your partner or a valued friend in such reflection.

Would it have been a good idea to have removed that distinctive silver-plated fish from the back panel of your automobile before berating the mechanic you felt had overcharged and underperformed in servicing your vehicle yesterday? Did you forget about those young ears listening from the backseat as you scolded your spouse for some comparatively insignificant matter on the drive to worship this morning? How would God rate in a neighbourhood opinion poll if those in your community made their judgment based solely on your outspokenness at the controversial community association meeting or the gathering for the community school parents the other evening?

Chapter Five: The Mess at Sodom

I am not asking you to focus only on a couple of rough days because we all have those. I am primarily interested in targeting the bigger picture of your reputation as a churchgoer or a religious person in your neighbourhood, your place of employment, your professional association or the minor sports programs where your children participate. If you claim to be a child of God, what do people conclude about the nature of your God by observing the way you live over a significant period of time?

The reason I pose such possibly uncomfortable questions is because it is inappropriate for us to reflect on the suggestion that God is loser friendly without engaging the fact that we are every bit as much a loser as any of the characters in Genesis. We ought to never lose sight of the reality that we too have as many shortcomings as that individual we dismiss as a loser at work, the gym, the church, or on the freeway.

Sure, we can read the stories in the Bible, peruse the words I am writing here, shake our heads at both the gravity of the sin we observe and the comparative marvel of God's grace. We can even derive personal encouragement and comfort from the recognition that God is truly loser friendly. But I want to push you a bit further. Merely reading the text does not automatically translate to mean that we have mastered the implications of the text.

If, as we are identifying in these pages, God is loser friendly, then what are the personal implications of that truth for my claim to be one of his children in terms of my being friendly and gracious to fellow losers? After all, should not the child resemble the Father in this manner at least to some extent?

I am greatly challenged and rebuked by the example of Abraham in this respect as we find his behaviour recorded in the latter part of Genesis 18. If we were too hard on old Abe in a previous chapter, let us now do the responsible thing and extend full credit to him when it is merited.

Abraham is advised of what God is about to do in terms of destroying Sodom and Gomorrah. In light of what was mentioned earlier in this chapter about making an attempt to read the story without knowing what lies ahead, recall that all we have been told regarding Sodom so far in the text is that they "were sinning greatly against the Lord" (13:13). Any hint regarding the nature of that sin is not evident to readers until after Abraham's noteworthy attempt to intervene in what God was planning for these cities as it is revealed in 18:20f.

So, what was Abraham's reaction to God's communication to him regarding the latter's intent to destroy these communities? He pled with God for mercy and attempted to intervene on behalf of Sodom and Gomorrah is what he did (18:16–33).

Abraham's immediate response to the revelation was to ask God to spare Sodom and Gomorrah if even fifty innocent people could be found within the twin cities. The longer he thinks about it, he realizes he is going to be fortunate if he can scare up even ten innocent people in the area. Abraham then engages in a kind of garage sale bartering with God making it clear in the process that he was in no way rubbing his hands in glee at the prospect of the impending judgment on the people of Sodom and Gomorrah.

Abraham does not say, "What a great idea that is, God. Go ahead and wipe out those perverts. That will teach them. Can I rub the stones together to commence the conflagration? Please! These dudes have had this coming for a long, long time now."

Rather, Abraham is essentially on his knees in fervent prayer pleading that God hold back on his plans to destroy the cities. It is as if he is looking over God's shoulder saying "Are you really sure that is what you want to do to these guys? Perhaps there is an alternative solution, Lord."

Given the condemnatory rhetoric against homosexuals that is often heard today from those who purport to represent the Almighty's point of view, Abraham's example on the matter prompts both a pointed question and an honest answer.

It is one thing to gratefully declare based on what we see in Genesis that God is loser friendly. But that is really only one half of the issue. To make such an affirmation requires the corresponding question: am I similarly loser friendly?

Simply put: should not the children of a loser friendly God be loser friendly also? If we believe God has extended second, third and fourth chances to us in our lives, should we not find great delight in considering the possibility of his extending the same to other losers? Could it be that we are not truly loser friendly until we learn to intercede and intervene on behalf of other sinners with a similar intensity that Abraham demonstrated in his passion to have Sodom and Gomorrah spared God's judgment?

To press this thought even further as it impacts the modern context, consider the wrongdoing of Sodom and Gomorrah from the traditional perspective that homosexuality was rampant in these cities. Are we as outspoken in our intercession for today's homosexuals as we are in our condemnation of them? What might Abraham say to us if he were able to frankly address us on that matter?

One of the everyday elements of life in North America that I find most disquieting has to do with the deep rifts being created in society by the irresponsible rhetoric now being dispensed via the comparative anonymity of social media. It has recently come to the fore most noticeably in the political sphere. Disagree with the President of the United States and you must be an irrational liberal. Agree with him and it is certain you are a rabid fascist. In such a tainted environment, civil discourse is increasingly difficult to find as is any trace of compassion for fellow citizens.

Unfortunately, the same kind of absurd rationale has trickled into the Church world. Say something critical of the gay community and you are immediately labelled homophobic or a gay basher by some. Challenge some of the vehemence with which homosexuals are denounced by some professing Christians and you will be accused of being spineless and soft on moral issues or labelled a compromiser who refuses to take a bold stand for righteousness and the clarity of the inspired Word of God.

One characteristic of the church constituency that annoys me to no end is how selective some of us can be when reading Scripture. I have had members approach me in every congregation where I have been a pastor encouraging me to preach against homosexuality based on St. Paul's words found in 1 Corinthians 6:9ff. I usually begin my response by telling them that I am not a big fan of topical sermons. (Indeed, Dr. Walter Kaiser, Jr., my former seminary professor that I have previously referred to and quoted from, used to advise us to: "Preach a topical sermon once every five years and then immediately get down on your knees and ask God for forgiveness"). Amen.

In the interests of accurately handling the Scripture, I have attempted to honour the intent of that directive throughout my career by always preaching the Scripture within the broader context of the literary unit in which it is located. That means there is no hopscotching in the same sermon from an Old Testament historical book to a New Testament epistle then into the apocalyptic daze of Revelation then into the satire of Ecclesiastes for me.

Once I have settled that matter with those seeking a specific sermon of their choosing, I will proceed to explain to those looking for a good old fashioned "hang 'em over hellfire" rant against homosexuality that I may consider doing so, but only after I have given equal attention to each of the other sins listed by St. Paul in the text that they have, thank you very much, brought to my attention.

"Do any of you struggle with adultery, idolatry, theft, greed, alcohol abuse, slander, or extortion?" I will ask. From the responses I receive, you would think it was a rhetorical question. I remember a deacon's meeting at one church where, as we stuffed our faces with large wedges of chocolate cake washed down by ample amounts of caffeine, we pondered the suitability of appointing a particular individual in the fellowship as a new deacon given that he was known to enjoy a glass of wine with his dinner. "Somebody

Chapter Five: The Mess at Sodom

see that that European gets saved, bless God!" was the sentiment that prevailed.

Really, people? Will somebody, please, anybody, just introduce some levity into such self-righteous gatherings to level the legalism and lock-up the loopholes on such nonsense?

When I turn the question back on zealous congregants in such a manner, it is usually sufficient to make them cool their jets for a spell. Often they will give me a quizzical look suggesting my orthodoxy should definitely be up for review before uttering some self-serving variation of what the people of Athens said to St. Paul as recorded in Acts 17:18–20: "What is this babbler trying to say? … You are bringing some strange ideas to our ears, and we want to know what they mean."

There are some key lessons about attitudes toward the gay community that the ardent gatekeepers of public morality need to learn from the interaction between Abraham and God in this account. Chief among them is that being loser friendly or sinner friendly is not tantamount to condoning wrongdoing. Jesus had much to say for believers to absorb and emulate in this regard. He demonstrated that, in fact, to be sinner friendly is one of the most profound evidences we can exhibit to demonstrate that we are indeed on God's side when it comes to being loser friendly.

Always remember that it was the zealous members of the religious elite of Christ's day that had minimal use for his penchant to hang out with and engage those of ill repute. As just one example, check out the crowd's response in Luke 19:7 to Christ's words to Zacchaeus one day indicating that he wished to spend some time at his home in Jericho.

In light of this, I ask you even as I again ask myself: when was the last time that like Abraham, we humbly (note verse 27's "I am but dust and ashes") and persistently (Forty? Thirty? Twenty? Ten?) interceded on behalf of those we consider among the most obstinate or vile of losers and sinners? When was the last time any one of us meaningfully engaged in friendship with someone who has different views and practices than we do with regard to any component of the profoundly complex matter of human sexuality?

Followers of a loser friendly God should be constantly motivated and characterized by God's patience

It is apparent from what we are told in Genesis 19 that Lot, despite being warned of the impending destruction of Sodom and Gomorrah, was in no immediate hurry to leave town (see 19:15 "at dawn the next day" ... Lot wanted to sleep on it ... vs. 16 "Lot still hesitated" to the point where the angels had to grab him and literally drag him out of the city; even then he wants to argue about where he was going to go).

I am going to venture that some of us can be much like Lot along this line. Our zeal can be misplaced when it comes to being slow to disassociate from iniquity. We can smugly assume that our wrongdoing is slightly less abhorrent or slightly more tolerable than the next guy's. We can be inclined to take our jolly time in acting on God's clear prompting, second guessing the Almighty and those who would caution us of impending consequence. However, the more I reflect on the practical ramifications of this story for me, I am afraid I must confess that I can often be much less patient and tolerant than God demonstrated at Sodom and Gomorrah. Had I been God, it would have been a matter of, "Ok, Lot, you don't want to leave this hell-hole? Watch this!"

But God is apparently more longsuffering than most of us; he is truly not willing that any should perish (2 Peter 3:9). He patiently waits until Lot is safely out of town before destruction rains down. Any professed devotee to a loser friendly God has to be both impressed and instructed by the demonstration of God's astonishing tolerance that is displayed in this story.

We learn later in Scripture that there were additional problems in Sodom and Gomorrah than the evil usually associated with its name. In Ezekiel 16:48f, the prophet rails against Jerusalem for its wickedness by saying: "Sodom was never as wicked as you are. The sins of Sodom were pride, laziness and gluttony, while the poor and needy suffered outside her door. She was proud and did loathsome things, so I wiped her out, as you have seen."

However, since the homosexuality aspect of Sodom and Gomorrah's disrepute still earns significant attention from certain quarters of the religious community in our day, as I conclude this chapter I want you to think with me concerning how people of faith ought to react to the issues of sexuality and gender that have become so controversial in modern North American society.

As you know, we live in a prolonged period of what has been named "the culture wars." Prominent and public agitation challenging conventional beliefs about human sexuality have been common since approximately the 1960s. From those early days of protest in favour of gay rights, we are now living in an era where the lines are being strategically blurred with respect to gender identity and rights. In response to these developments, many communities of faith have taken it upon themselves to politicize morality.

The rise of The Moral Majority in the U.S. in the 1970s was one of the best examples of this trend. Today, Christians in America are sharply divided by what, as I noted earlier, I call "American religitics." I readily acknowledge a studied skepticism regarding much of the thinking that fuels the heated rhetoric that has characterized American religio-politico interaction over the past almost fifty years.

With all due respect to the earnest architects of the American dream, I have come to reject the notions—some would call them doctrines—of "American exceptionalism" and "manifest destiny" that posit a unique role for the United States of America in the thinking and acting of the Almighty. I consider such a self-serving and historically myopic perspective responsible for much of the nonsense that prevails today in American public discourse or "religitics."

At no point in Scripture do I see God's modern people being called to primarily establish a political identity or become completely preoccupied with enforcing their role as salt and light via political means. Despite the modern complexities of the nation-state world that has evolved since Abraham's day, I am resolute in my rejection of anything that suggests the kingdom of God will triumph as the result of the political instrumentation of any one modern nation or group of nations.

Tom Sine hits the nail on the head in this regard when he observes:

> It is clear, therefore, that there is nothing in either Scripture or history to support the contention that America is God's new chosen nation, God's special agent to save the world. That is the role of the church. Regrettably, some leaders of the religious right do history the way cult leaders do theology: they select bits and pieces of history and arrange them in ways that support the positions they want to prove. The result is no longer history but mythology. Perhaps the most troubling aspect of this myth-making is that it has drawn many sincere Christians to unwittingly embrace another faith and serve another god." (Sine, 1995, p. 125)

Those of us next door in Canada are often able to detect a ripple or runoff effect from such that shows up in the thinking of some believers in our country as well. Religious belief has thus become so politicized that at times it can be virtually impossible to determine where matters of religion end and issues of politics begin or vice-versa.

I have no particular interest in minimizing the legitimate concerns of people of faith as they relate to the culture wars. I do, however, think there is a significant amount of wisdom in observing what Abraham did and what he did not do as it concerned the situation at Sodom and Gomorrah. His behaviour in this regard is some-

Chapter Five: The Mess at Sodom

thing I believe modern believers do well to receive and replicate in both our thought and conduct today.

What was Abraham's response to the homosexuality and assorted wickedness of Sodom and Gomorrah?

Did he organize an economic or politically motivated boycott of local merchants? Did he distribute pamphlets warning of judgement or hold rallies and press conferences declaring AIDS to be God's judgment on homosexuals? Did he petition the government to do something about gay perverts and pass legislation to stem their influence on impressionable children? Did he convene a conference on the threat posed to his promised family by those caught up in an alternative lifestyle?

No. And, trust me, I'm not intending to oversimplify or minimize the complexity of the issues to which I have just made passing reference. Please hear the point I wish to make. Notice, instead, what Abraham did, in fact, undertake because I believe it is profound in its simplicity and is something that is missing from much of the rhetoric and activity associated with modern culture wars.

He focused his attention and energy on persistently petitioning for mercy on behalf of those apparently deserving of God's judgement.

I can already here the reactions and objections from some of you. "That's too simplistic!" "That does not take into account the significant theological, cultural and political differences and realities that must be addressed in the complex twenty-first century nation-state in which we live!" "Did Jesus not command that we are to be salt and light in decaying and dark times?"

Believe me, I have heard most of the relevant and usually angry comebacks from energized Christians on these issues over the course of my career as a pastor and a commentator-journalist in mainstream media. I have had passionate people call my church, e-mail me or stop me at the shopping centre to express extreme displeasure at something I have written or said in the public domain on a hot social topic. Some have called my home and unleashed their displeasure on my children upon learning I was not at home.

God bless such zeal. The stupidity, not so much.

I wish here to simply register that most of us are usually more adept at energetically vocalizing our views to whomever will give us an ear than we are at doggedly engaging in fervent prayer to seek God's restraint and compassion on those who are in our ideological cross-hairs.

Abraham was to become the father of many nations and religions. His example in this regard is therefore of essential consequence even amidst the turbulence of the culture wars taking place in the complicated times we are experiencing in twenty-first century North America. I therefore simply affirm the wisdom of another old-timer, Donald Grey Barnhouse, who once penned: "Never are we more like Christ than when we are interceding" (Barnhouse, 1973, p. 156).

Chapter Six:
Laughter; Or Not
(Genesis 26:1–28:9)

When we try to see a damaged person as one of God's regular old customers, instead of a lost cause, it takes the pressure off everybody. We can then loosen our death grip on the person, which usually is progress for everybody, also known in certain circles as grace.
(Anne Lamott, 2013, pp. 67–68)

It is not at all difficult for me to imagine that in the immediate aftermath of "the bizarre incident," as it came to be called, whenever he walked the corridors of the local elementary school, other young people would point their fingers at him and whisper behind their hands. "That's him! Isaac! Word is the Child Welfare people showed up at his place the other day and took him away from that elderly couple he denies are his grandparents although they are certainly old enough to be such!"

"Huh? Why? What did he do?"

"It's not so much a matter of what he did, as what his old man is said to have done. Witnesses say a couple of weeks ago that old geezer Abraham took the kid up into the mountains, tied him up on a pile of rocks and threatened to kill him with a dagger. The crazy old coot claims he would have done it too had not God told him at the last second to stop. Can you believe it? Talk about a nut job! So, Child Welfare pays them all a visit the other day and takes Isaac away for questioning. Seems they're thinking maybe Abraham is in the early stages of dementia or perhaps he's just getting a little carried away with his religious beliefs."

Given that we live in times when news of children being removed from homes owing to the incompetence of their parent(s), foster parent(s) or guardian(s) is not at all unusual, I find it a challenge to avoid reading the story of Abraham's aborted sacrifice of Isaac through the filter of modern media reports. Add to this the likelihood that many of today's child psychologists would propose that, given the abusive trauma Isaac was exposed to in his early years, he should definitely be excused for leading a life that really did not amount to much.

I do not claim to fully comprehend all of the ethical, moral and theological questions that arise from this most curious of stories about an event that occurred sometime during Isaac's early years. (Given that his name meant "he laughs," did Isaac at the time somehow think the entire episode was Abraham's idea of a joke? "Ha, ha, Dad, you're such a joker. Right, Dad? Uh, Dad! You're just kidding, right? Dad? DAD!!"

Enns and Byas see theological significance in this incident via their approach of allowing later texts such as Exodus 13 and Numbers 8 to influence the interpretation of God testing Abraham in Genesis 22 utilizing an awareness that "The firstborn of every womb, animal or human, belongs to Yahweh." They also point out that "...[T]he larger point of this story, from a later Israelite point of view is this: Israel is, was, and always will be God's firstborn son (Exodus 4:22) and is, was, and always will be safe in God's hands—no matter how dire the circumstances" (Enns & Byas, p. 76).

In any case, on the basis of this incident alone, I am inclined to be sympathetic as to why the larger story of Isaac in Genesis reveals a somewhat dysfunctional if not, disturbed, individual. Assuming that by the conclusion of the event where Abraham appeared truly ready to sacrifice his long-anticipated son, Isaac realized that Abraham was indeed serious, I am more than willing to cut Isaac some slack for a kind of Post Traumatic Stress Disorder that followed him into his marriage and on into his senior years.

Chapter Six: Laughter; Or Not

The shadow of his father, Abraham, looms large over the narrative of Isaac's life in Genesis, graphically verifying the validity of the popular axiom: "like father, like son." As was the case with his old man, throughout his life Isaac similarly reflected certain attitudes and attributes that we might say contribute to designating someone a loser.

What then might modern readers discover in this most unusual of stories that may be of some benefit to us?

Two questions

Upon engaging the comparatively brief Genesis record of Isaac's life there are two queries that immediately traverse to the forefront of my thinking.

The first has to do with pondering what kind of a behavioural legacy I as a father am in the process of leaving for my children and/or grandchildren. In reading the story of Isaac, it is sobering yet prudent for any parent to reflect on what the experts are known to advise regarding how the lessons our children learn from us are more often caught than taught.

One of the finest pieces of popular musical artistry I have encountered in my lifetime that capably articulates the essence of this vital matter is the song *Cat's in the Cradle* popularized over more than four decades ago by the late American musician, Harry Chapin. If you are so young that you do not recognize either the artist or the song, stop reading immediately and go to your computer. Access YouTube and enter "Harry Chapin Cat's in the Cradle" (Harry Chapin & Sandy Chapin, 1974). Trust me, doing so is absolutely essential to assisting you in comprehending the gravity of the point I wish to establish here.

(Pause while you go to your computer.)

And now you know why the song is legendary.

So far in our look at the contents of Genesis, Isaac has more or less been in the background. The spotlight has been focused on his parents along with Hagar and Ishmael before shifting to Rebekah, the woman selected to be his wife. Curiously enough, we are even introduced to Isaac's squabbling offspring (end of chapter 25) before we really get much by way of insight into the character of Isaac himself. For an individual who figured so prominently in the drama of the early chapters of Genesis that portray Abraham and Sarah, apart from the story of Abraham's aborted sacrifice of him, there is minimal information given us about Isaac's life prior to his advanced years of deteriorating health.

And what do we find in the brief insights that we are given concerning Isaac?

Well, we find him telling strangers that his wife is his sister (26:7–11). Oops. Déjà vu! Is Isaac borrowing a trick from the stories he had heard from his father Abraham about earlier years? Or should this be seen more in line with the suggestion of some scholars as evidence that there are several authors in evidence throughout Genesis?

What I find both interesting and instructive in the story of Isaac as it stands is that whereas there were likely many commendable qualities about Abraham that were passed on to Isaac which the author(s) of Genesis might have related, the sparse information that is conveyed concerning him such as this incident does not present either Abraham or Isaac in a very favourable light.

Isaac is portrayed as a diligent agriculturalist best known for being dishonest regarding the identity of his wife and for playing favourites with his children. In what borders on some kind of tragic comedy, he ends up being deceived by one of his sons who operates in tandem with Rebekah in an incident that in our modern culture might qualify as senior abuse. Isaac comes across as little more than a confused geriatric who cannot see very well in more ways than one. There really is not much material here that could be used in putting together a complimentary video tribute for the guy's funeral, is there?

He is essentially presented as bumbling about picking up where his father left off with respect to honing his skills of deception. No sooner does God inform Isaac in the opening verse of chapter 26 of his impending greatness than Isaac attempts to manipulate King Abimelech to ensure that such does indeed happen.

Abraham lied and deceived, and Isaac sets out to carry on the family tradition. Further, as we will see, under the skilled tutelage of Isaac's wife, Rebekah, his youngest son, Jacob, proceeds to turn deception into an art form. Uncle Laban would soon verify that Jacob was indeed doomed from both sides of the gene pool when it came to being a master of deceit.

Boom! Double whammy!

It makes me wonder what family reunions were like when Jacob and Uncle Laban were in attendance. "Oh-oh. Hide your valuables, family. Both Jacob and Uncle Laban are planning to attend Dad and Mom's 95th wedding anniversary." Do you think competitions were held at Isaac and Rebekah's family events each year to determine who would win the Best Rip-Off Artist award?

Ha, once again, bear in mind that it is comparatively easy to point the finger at these ancient figures and pinpoint their faults all the while being guilty of overlooking or minimizing our own. Too easy.

Each of our children participated in numerous minor sports during their growing-up years. At one point all three of them were participating in soccer which I have subsequently learned is reportedly North America's fastest growing sport.

Following one busy Saturday of chasing around with the kids from one soccer pitch to the next, my wife confronted me after they had been put to bed for the night. "What did you say to your oldest son about the refereeing at his game?" she accused with the subtlety of an avalanche.

Distressed by yet another failure on my beloved's behalf to grant me the deference, yea indeed, to credit me with the esteem an ordained minister works so diligently to acquire, I submitted an evasive response. "Why do you ask?" "Because," she offered, noticeably elevating the intensity of her inquiry, "both of your sons are referring to the referees using terms that I know full well they heard from you!"

"Honey, honey," I protested, kissing her cheek, "it has been a long day. You know as well as I do that the boys have been spending too much time over at that Jeff kid's house. I believe his parents are Presbyterians, aren't they? Our boys are simply picking up the loose language for which theological liberals like that are so renowned."

Given what we see in the story of Isaac regarding how behavioural tendencies are transferred from one generation to the next, every parent does well to periodically ask ourselves as to the behavioural legacy we will leave our children. Again, just do it!

The second question that comes to my mind in reading the Isaac narrative prompts me to wonder concerning how my own insecurities and fears impair my faith.

Even though we are given only a small amount of information concerning Isaac's life, it is apparent that much of it was controlled by fear. Another character trait learned from Abraham? In the early verses of Genesis 26, the Lord appears to Isaac to confirm the oath the Almighty had given his father, Abraham: "I will make your descendants as numerous as the stars in the sky ... and through your offspring all nations on earth will be blessed" (vs. 4).

Just three verses later, however, when asked about the identity of his wife, Isaac maintains that Rebekah was his sister "because he was afraid to say, 'she is my wife.'" "The men of this place might kill me," Isaac concedes before confessing his angst yet again in verse 9 by admitting "I thought I might lose my life on account of her."

God repeatedly advises characters in the Bible who were called upon to serve him in some significant way to "fear not" (26:24). On some occasions it was an angel that communicated this directive. Similarly, Jesus frequently said the same to his disciples throughout the course of his time on earth, "do not be afraid."

God is obviously aware that fear presents a primary impairment to humankind's ability to exercise faith. Fear restricts our aptitude to be all that God intends us to be and to do all that God intends us to do. Fear not only impairs faith but, at times, extinguishes it. That is one of the reasons Jesus encouraged his followers to "be of good cheer," not "of good fear." It is an instruction that modern Christ followers are wise to keep in the forefront of our minds. I consider it shameful when pastors and other preachers consciously employ fear to elicit support for some of our half-baked theological notions.

Just as one's capacity to operate a motor vehicle is impaired by the consumption of alcohol, so too a believer's ability to appropriately exercise faith is impaired when we are absorbed with fear. While there may be no such thing as perfect faith, of course, it is beneficial to recognize that one takes a big step in the right direction when we learn to identify and deal with the fear factor in our efforts to walk by faith.

Frederick Buechner offers his usual erudite insight here when he contrasts the comparatively messy nature of faith to other aspects of attempting to live in relationship to God such as theology, mysticism, ethics and worship:

> Faith ... is distinctly different from other aspects of the Christian life and not to be confused with them ... Faith is closest perhaps to worship because like worship it is essentially a response to God and involves the emotions and the physical senses as well as the mind, but worship is consistent, structured, single-minded and seems to know what it's doing while faith is a stranger and exile on the earth and doesn't know for certain about anything. Faith is homesickness. Faith is a lump in the throat. Faith is less a position *on* than a movement *toward*, less a sure thing than a hunch. Faith is waiting. Faith is journeying through space and through time. (Buechner, 2006, pp. 172–173) (emphasis original)

Isaac actually takes a big step forward by discerning and acknowledging that it is fear that limits his faith. No doubt he speaks for many of us in this respect. Fear can freeze faith and leave us immobilized, dissatisfied and unproductive on our spiritual journey.

Are you allowing fear to impose limitations on your faith today? Am I permitting fear to sabotage my trust in God? Are we willing to exercise the necessary honesty to identify such to ourselves, to a trusted fellow believer, to God? Or do we even fear the possibility of someone thinking less of us for admitting to our feebleness of faith?

God's response to Isaac's confession of fear is not to berate him or remind him that he is a loser. In the remainder of chapter 26 we see evidence that Isaac's life, similar to his father Abraham's experience, prospered in terms of material assets. So obvious was God's blessing in his life that even King Abimelech's agents were prompted to acknowledge: "'"We saw clearly that the Lord was with you ...You are blessed by the Lord"'" (26:28, 29). Isaac's fears, like many of our own, proved to be unfounded.

If, as we have seen, Isaac's earthly father committed his fair share of blunders, his heavenly father proved abundantly gracious to him, saying at a strategic point in Isaac's life: "I am the God of your father Abraham. Do not be afraid, for I am with you; I will bless you and will increase the number of your descendants for the sake of my servant Abraham" (26:24).

Somewhat ironically, a man whose name means "laughter" or "he laughs" makes only a brief appearance on the Genesis stage. At that, it is really just long enough for us to comprehend the truth that ultimately life is no laughing matter. For sure, Sarah's ability to conceive at her advanced age merits a chuckle or two. But Isaac probably was not laughing as a young man when he saw his father raise an arm grasping a knife with the intent to terminate Isaac's life.

Fear seems to have kept Abraham's son from anything resembling an easygoing personality. Nor did he have much to smile about in his later years as his health deteriorated amidst the ethical and spiritual shenanigans perpetrated by his wife and their youngest son.

True, Isaac may have been named "laughter." Yet I cannot help but wonder if there may have been some times in his life when he wished that Abraham had gone ahead and finished him off on that occasion in his youth when they went for that stroll into the mountains of Moriah.

Chapter Seven:
She's Good With Camels, Not So Good With Children
(Genesis 25–27)

> *My mother almost never cried—her parents were English—so the Kleenex [in her purse] weren't to wipe tears; and she had drowned in those uncried tears. Uncried-tears syndrome left my mother hypervigilant, unable to settle down into herself, and—to use the clinical term—cuckoo.*
> (Anne Lamott, 2005, p. 49)

I had never heard of it until a few years ago. It is labelled Parental Alienation Syndrome (PAS) and it generated considerable controversy across North America for a time. In Alberta, where I live, a judge transferred custody of a four year old boy to a mother who charged that her ex-husband and ex-mother-in-law had maliciously turned her son against her and that the boy was suffering from PAS. In British Columbia, a woman who denied her husband access to their daughter for two years, lost custody of the nine-year old when lawyers successfully argued that the girl was, similarly, suffering from Parental Alienation Syndrome.

Dr. Richard Gardner, a researcher at Columbia University, says children can be brainwashed by a custodial parent into developing an irrational animosity for the other parent. Interestingly enough, the professor claims that women are responsible for 90% of serious PAS cases (Heitler, 2018).

I cannot help but think Rebekah may have been the original founder of the Parental Alienation Syndrome Association when I read about her in these chapters of Genesis. That's because it is evident she was a master of manipulation with a distinct ability to promote alienation in her own family. I would not want to have been in this lady's bad books because, for whatever reasons, she clearly had a few axes to grind with certain family members. (I encourage readers to check out Oprah Winfrey's delightful production *Greenleaf* on Netflix that lifts the lid on the mischief in a pastor's family in the American South. For several reasons, Rebekah kept coming to mind as I watched the work of the actress who plays the role of the bishop's wife in that revealing series.)

Rebekah's mastery at scheming is part of the reason why I am sincerely puzzled by Christian parents who choose to name their daughters, Rebekah. Really!? Have you actually read the entire story of Rebekah as conveyed in Genesis?

I will confess I have occasionally been known to politely tease some parents when they inform their pastor that they consider(ed) Rebekah in the Bible a good role model for their new baby. To this I sometimes respond: "Alright, so Rebekah is portrayed in Genesis as quite adept at watering camels and assorted domestic chores, but when was the last time you read the rest of her story? What do you see there that you want your daughter to emulate in her life? Which part of Rebekah's demeanor as a wife and mother jumped out at you from the pages of Genesis whereby you thought it a responsible act of piety to saddle your precious little girl with that name for the rest of her life?" Selah.

On occasion, my longsuffering parishioners have reconsidered and hastened down to the Department of Vital Statistics to change the baby's name to Delilah or Rahab. (You are right. I probably should be reported to the appropriate ecclesiastical authorities.)

Rebekah is another character from Genesis that seems to have a long history of being considered a suitable role model for Christian females. I grew up with several girls by that name and have met many others throughout my life who are so named. In point of fact, however, even the hastiest reviews of her story in the few chapters of Genesis where she appears indicate that Rebekah leaves much to be desired when it comes to some of the personal character traits she demonstrates. Nor does she come across as a paragon of what it means to live with a meaningful faith in God.

The primary point of my drawing attention to such a reality is not merely to beat up on Rebekah or on well-intentioned parents. Rather, it is to focus on yet another prime example from Genesis of the fact that God is loser friendly.

God chooses and uses people who are every bit as human, fallen, depraved and dysfunctional as you and I. In fact, we might be justified in advancing the prospect that, at times, God appears to severely limit himself owing to the foibles present in the lives of the quirky individuals in Genesis he calls to help effect his eternal plan and to function as his public relations team.

The only viable reason to be offered by way of justification for this puzzling characteristic of the Almighty is to underscore that he is a God of grace. He does not choose us because of our merit or for our spectacular skillsets. In short, we are seriously lacking with regard to living up to his lofty standards.

Are you beginning to see the portrait that emerges in Genesis? It's not about you! From the opening chapters of the Old Testament, not just as evidenced in the life of Jesus Christ and so vividly sketched in the New Testament, the God of the Bible is first and foremost a God of grace who chooses and loves people despite our persistent capacity to fail him.

Whatever readers of the Bible choose to do by way of attempting to accommodate the traditionally difficult sections of the Old Testament in which God is portrayed as unreasonably angry or inhumanely judgmental of mankind's faults, such needs to be undertaken only after giving adequate allowance to his grace that is portrayed over and over again in Genesis.

Some encouragement for anyone acquainted with parenthood

Since I graduated from seminary at Christmas 1984, I have witnessed what I believe church historians in years to come will document as some very crucial alterations in North American society. These, in turn, have had a profound influence on the implications for effective ministry in parish life. One of the areas in which change has occurred in what seems to me to be an almost 180-degree turnaround, has been with respect to domestic life: marriage, family and parenting issues.

Many of the familial assumptions a pastor could make when greeting visitors at the church door following worship services during the era that I emerged from my theological training cannot be made today. Trust me on this. I have won the Golden Foot in Mouth Award far too often over the past four decades to have my judgment questioned on this assessment.

In my early days in pastoral life, I could safely assume that the unknown man, woman and three children standing in front of me as they departed following worship constituted what was traditionally called a nuclear family unit. Any pastor making such assumptions today will soon qualify as a contender to imminently dethrone me as reigning champion of the Golden Foot in Mouth Award.

How many times in the late twentieth or early twenty-first centuries has my face turned crimson as, in response to my efforts to simply be friendly to newcomers, I have heard "Oh, no, this one is *his* son, and these two are *my* children," or a similar explanation regarding the identity of the children in the group? Further, on this topic, I will simply celebrate that I am also finally starting to comprehend that just because a person today is sporting a wedding band does not guarantee that any conclusions you make in that regard will necessarily be accurate. I recall a woman once informing me that, although she was indeed divorced, she was still wearing her band from her past marriage because God had assured her that the break-up would yet be healed and the marriage would flourish again. I am not inclined these days to question or challenge assertions regarding what the Almighty has affirmed to any hopeful soul.

In an era when families are upended, mended, blended and resplendid, let's now attempt to identify what there is of value that can be salvaged from what we see in the life of Rebekah as she is depicted in Genesis.

A mother's role is one of the most important and difficult of tasks

It is common every spring around Mother's Day to encounter news articles or business reports reminding us of a mother's value to society in economic terms. Because we live in a capitalist society (IN GOLD WE TRUST), it often takes seeing a mother's worth spelled out in terms of dollars and cents for it to appropriately register with us just how essential the role is that mothers have in our society.

Valerie Young speaks to this in an informative article that appeared in *Brain Child* magazine:

> Mothers make people, and people are the most basic economic element. Babies are consummate consumers. They grow to be producers—of everything! Without children, there is no economy, and no future. We know that the value of family care to elders saves public spending and, if compensated, would be worth around $450 billion a year. The US economy's GDP for 2014 is estimated at upwards of $17 trillion. If mothers' uncompensated labour – in birthing, nursing, and raising children, and the myriad activities that involves—were tallied up, estimates place its value at between 21% and 50% of GDP. Nancy Folbre, a Professor of Economics at UMass Dartmouth and frequent past contributor to the *New York Times Economix* blog, places a conservative estimate at 25% of GDP. So that means that mothers' unpaid domestic labor actually adds between $4 trillion and $8.5 trillion to the economy. Every. Year. (Young, 2015)

Wow! Pay attention the next time the mother of your children mentions that her invoice is in the mail.

Consider another perspective on the topic that humorously but accurately encapsulates Mom's imperative place in the life of a family:

> Here, according to another writer are 52 "job titles" a mom holds on any given day:
>
> 1) CEO of the Household; 2) Personal Chef (clients may consist of picky eaters); 3) Head Cheerleader of (insert your child's name) team; 4) Housekeeper; 45) Taxi Driver (don't expect to receive any tips); 6) Judge Mom (daily court appearances); 7) PhD in Anger Management; 8) Hair Stylist (mostly consists of impatient clients); 9) Bed-wetting Patrol Squad; 10) Keeper of Secrets (shhh, I won't tell); 11) Food Tester; 12) Family Therapist (innervations at least once a week); 13) Toddler Wrestling Coach; 14) Errand Runner; 15) Laundry Machine Operator; 16) Janitor; 17) Teacher (specializing in nursery rhymes, ABC's and 123's); 18) Toy Repair Expert (fixer of the little parts); 19) Finance Manager; 20) Art Director (remember; beauty is in the eye of the beholder); 21) Land Scraper (the weeds won't pull themselves); 22) Potty Trainer; 23) Search and Rescue (for lost toys); 24) Champion Tickler; 25) Lifeguard; 26) Daycare Provider; 27) Personal Assistant for the entire family; 28) No-Thumb Sucking Enforcer; 29) Wardrobe Stylist (this may consist of changing your client's clothes several times a day); 30) Personal Shopper; 31) Toothbrush Inspector; 32) PTA Mom; 33) Play-date Coordinator; 34) Birthday Events Director; 35) Sleep Scientist (will consist of many overnight studies); 36) Scary Monster Patrol Officer; 37) Dramatic Story Teller 38) Backyard Safety Patrol; 39) Professional Singer (concentrating on lullabies); 40) Boo-Boo Fixer; 41) Kiss and Hugs Expert; 42) Speech Specialist; 43) Vacation Coordinator & Tour Guide; 44) PhD in Reverse Psychology; 45) Sepa-

ration Anxiety Counselor; 46) In-Law Mediator; 47) Seamstress of Frilly Dresses and Super Hero Costumes; 48) Mrs. Fix-It; 49) Fort Engineer; 50) Stain Removal Expert; 51) Bodyguard; 52) Lady MacGyver; (Seitzinger, 2011)

I will let you add a few more jobs required of Moms from your own unique experiences.

What is of particular import here is that, as with any mother, there were myriad responsibilities and expectations that would have been placed on Rebekah. She was the mother of twins as well and therefore faced with all the additional challenges that reality presents.

So before we begin to critique Rebekah, it is useful to pause and at least give her the courtesy of recognizing that being a mother is a most demanding task and that, contrary to what popular capitalist society would have us believe, it is a responsibility far more important than we usually acknowledge.

Do you think parents living in Rebekah's day ever had to put up with listening to their children complain that "there is nothing to do?" Or is that just a phenomenon of the modern era?

When our children were small and would predictably lament the lack of adequate entertainment options, I would sometimes take them by the hand into the family room and show them a well-stocked bookcase, a computer, one of several televisions attached to which were any number of Sony PlayStation or Nintendo consoles. We would then proceed into the garage where an assortment of bicycles, snowboards, rollerblades, cleats, skates and numerous pieces of equipment for every sport imaginable were to be found collecting dust. I would then declare to them: "If I hear any one of you again complain that there is nothing to do, I will personally package you up in a wooden crate containing an active hornets' nest and return you to your manufacturer via the bumpiest ox-cart ride you have ever experienced! Are there any questions? I didn't think so."

All parents know with certainty that their role is not an easy one to wisely carry out! Are things any better or any worse today than the frustrations faced by parents in the days of Isaac and Rebekah? I will gladly permit you to address that question.

That is because of the contents of Genesis 25:22–23 where we read that Rebekah was not even permitted to wait until her twins were toddlers before she was schooled in the meaning of sibling rivalry. She was informed by the Lord while Esau and Jacob were yet in-utero that she was essentially nurturing the founding members of World Wrestling Entertainment. Do you think she slept well after coming home from the initial ultrasound with the Lord's words lingering in her ears: "Two nations are in your womb, and two peoples from within you will be separated; one people will be stronger than the other, and the older will serve the younger?"

So, again, as I suggested with respect to Sarah, we need to cut a dear lady some slack, okay? Her first pregnancy was not an easy one. Evidently, the battle line between her sons was drawn even before her water broke. As proof of that reality, Jacob was grasping Esau's heel at delivery as if to hold him back and enable himself to be born first. An indication of troubled days ahead.

Sibling rivalry has apparently been around a while, yes? It is certainly a repeated theme in Genesis: Cain and Abel; Esau and Jacob; Leah and Rachel; Joseph and his brothers. Rebekah's task as family referee began out of necessity shortly after Esau's head crowned at birth.

In an entertaining book titled *Born to Rebel: Birth Order, Family Dynamics and Creative Lives*, researcher Frank J. Sulloway reports evidence demonstrating that the oldest child in a family often tends to support the status quo. Those who are born later are more apt to show signs of rebellion and pursue innovative patterns of behaviour (Sulloway, 1997). Did Rebekah have any such resources to turn to for help in trying to understand the unique temperaments of her twins?

Perhaps the unique challenges of parenting twins can be seen as Esau and Jacob enter the Genesis narrative. Esau earns his father's approval and appears content to prepare to take over the family farm from Dad. Conversely, Jacob was inclined to be more of the quiet type who hung around the house. He was ever-thinking (scheming!), reflecting, cooking up menu items including how he might creatively outsmart his older brother and seize the birthright which he had already made a bold attempt to earn at birth.

No doubt mothering these two would have been a most challenging task. So again, let us hasten to give Rebekah an A+ for Effort.

A mother's influence is always powerful

Genesis 25:28 advises readers that Isaac and Rebekah each had their favourite son. As just mentioned, Isaac's preference was for Esau, a skillful hunter, apparently because Isaac had a particular appetite for wild game. On the other hand, Jacob enjoyed a close relationship with his mother, Rebekah, possibly because he seems to have been more domestically inclined. Beyond this small amount of information, however, we are left to speculate as to how or why this set of parents allowed familial relationships to develop in this manner.

The first real insight we are given concerning the lives of the twins after their birth begins in 25:29 where we find Jacob manipulating Esau out of the latter's birthright, that culture's traditional means of giving legal priority to the firstborn male. Esau returns famished from a strenuous hunting trip—his hunger likely enhanced by the aroma of the stew Jacob is preparing. (Here is that hunger motif again that we observed in Chapter Three with respect to Abraham's indiscretion. Now you know why experts advise us not to shop for groceries just before a meal—that is how and when poor decisions are made). Esau's hunger renders him particularly vulnerable to Jacob's scheme.

Beyond the fact that Jacob masterfully manipulates his older brother's appetite in order to swindle Esau's birthright, there are a couple of important questions we ought to ask at this point in an effort to fully grasp what ultimately transpires in this account and Rebekah's part in it.

For one thing, we could be excused for concluding from this story that God, on occasion, appears to be dependent on the deceitful and manipulative self-interests of his children in order to accomplish his overarching objectives. As we have already learned, the Lord had told Rebekah that the older twin would end up serving the younger one. Yet what are we to make of the manner in which that dynamic in Esau and Jacob's relationship comes about?

Marianne Meye Thompson's candor is helpful here in struggling with this component of the story. Her answer, while somewhat inconclusive regarding God's *modus operandi*, is as tenable a solution to an interesting dilemma as I have encountered:

> ...[That Rebekah] mak[es] this happen through deceiving an old, infirm man and cheating the older brother is puzzling...[W]hen I look at the entire narrative, I'm not so much bothered as intrigued by the way God's purpose is hinted at both in the selection of Rebekah as the wife of Isaac and in the somewhat mysterious oracle to Rebekah during her very difficult pregnancy... There's an acceptance of these characters, warts and all, and God chooses and works through and with them. That seems to be the writer's point. He doesn't need to make the characters look better." (Moyers, (Ed.), pp. 251–252)

It is perhaps at this stage in the story that some of us become uneasy. If, as we are seeing, God in his wisdom has elected to allow fallible human beings to have a primary role in accomplishing his purposes in this world, it is inevitable that at times God will appear to fall victim to the very inequities that are inherent in the humanity of his chosen instruments. That means there will be occasions such

Chapter Seven: She's Good With Camels, Not So Good With Children

as this one when it appears to us that God uses and even blesses deviant behaviour.

Any attempt to satisfactorily resolve all of the uncertainties and discomforts arising from such an assertion is certain to have its weaknesses. That is why I appreciate that an awareness of such is at least evident in separate comments made respectively by Robin Darling Young, Leon R. Kass and Naomi H. Rosenblatt in the Moyers PBS panel discussion:

> Sometimes God's plot seems to be advanced by deception, by stepping outside the apparent borders of what is acceptable so that life may go on.
>
> If this were a story by Machiavelli, we would think nothing of the deception because necessity requires it. But the Bible tells you by subsequent stories that even if the deception is necessary, it's unsavoury and you pay for it.
>
> The whole story of Genesis, from Abraham on, is really a saga of four generations in a family that some today might call 'dysfunctional.' But in the end, what we always have to get to is the larger vision of the story—that the family revolves around a covenant, and that the covenant becomes the common denominator that holds them all together and allows them to prevail and transcend. As long as they transmit that, they have vitality and a sense of purpose, meaning and values. (Moyers, (Ed.), p. 272)

There is a second question that begs to be addressed in this narrative. Where do you think Jacob got the genetic inclination that prompted him to take advantage of people, kicking the other guy when he is down and manipulating people so as to get his own way?

Given what Genesis 26:28 tells us about Jacob's lifestyle, it is fair to suggest that Jacob had likely spent significant time in his mother's presence. Therefore, based on Rebekah's deceitful actions in chapter 27 where she masterminds a plot to deceive her own husband so that Jacob fraudulently obtains his father's blessing, is it unfair to suggest that Jacob's penchant for deceit may have simply been his putting into practice what he had often seen and heard from his own mother during his formative years?

Rebekah shows no hesitation whatsoever in chapter 27 in directing Jacob to betray his older brother, deceive his father and even to cite the sovereignty of God (vs. 20) as an accessory to their dishonest scheme. On the basis of the example that his mother set with respect to deceiving people, can we be surprised that Jacob turns out to be the shyster he proves to be for most of his life?

A parent's influence is always very, very powerful, which is why it is beneficial for any responsible mother or father to regularly give serious thought to the matter of how we are influencing our children. Do we truly grasp the truth of the assertion that our actions ultimately speak much louder than our words?

My tenure in parish life has coincided with a couple of very interesting and controversial developments in the evolution of human sexuality. On the one hand, there has been a groundswell in popular culture to accept homosexuality as a legitimate form of sexual orientation and expression. In more recent years, a lobby has similarly begun to vocalize to recognize and accept that a percentage of the population now identifies as trans-gender (Tom, 2018).

Simultaneously, there has been a strong lobby by some sectors in society to advocate for abstinence as the superior and only permissible form of birth control for adolescents. Teenagers have been encouraged to sign covenants affirming their intention to refrain from sexual activity until marriage. For a time, devoted parents purchased purity rings for their teens to wear as a sign of their commitment in this regard. Behind this effort was a parental mindset communicating: "We need to tell our young people to just say 'no' to sexual promiscuity, just as we tell them to 'just say no' to drugs, alcohol and tobacco. In an age of permissiveness, our young people must be taught to practice restraint!"

Chapter Seven: She's Good With Camels, Not So Good With Children

I have frequently been asked for my perspective as a pastor on these issues and, with respect to the evolution of the latter, have also been asked to promote such initiatives. I fully understand the legitimate concerns parents have along this line for they are similar to the ones I had when our children were going through their teenage years.

How grateful I was and am for the solid counsel I have encountered from wise Christian thinkers and writers that enables me to respond something like this: "That is all very commendable, parents. But hey, Dad and Mom, how often do your children see you actually practice restraint? How often do they observe (not just hear) you 'just saying no' in your own lives as their primary Christian role models? Or are you guilty of failing to set a clear example concerning the kind of restraint you are expecting and demanding from them?"

I recently learned that the average Canadian spends on average something like $1.68 for every dollar we earn. I am no economist but that suggests to me that many of us are regularly succumbing to the non-stop demand from popular culture to upgrade this and renovate that. Apparently, we exercise minimal restraint before obtaining the new iPhone, a new Smart TV, the latest model vehicle or adding that mid-winter vacation to that favourite sun spot, all conveniently financed on our almost maximized credit cards.

It is the apex of foolishness to tell our children one thing while simultaneously practicing the polar opposite within their field of vision and hearing. We should be the first people to know that our children are more intelligent than that. Check it out in the New Testament—Jesus spent far more time talking about matters of mammon or money than he did about issues related to sexuality. Why have we so self-righteously overlooked, neglected and/or reversed this in our manner of Christian parenting?

By all means, go ahead and have those serious discussions with your children about sexual matters. But better yet, how about if you model restraint for them by showing some of it when it comes to the material things that we adults find so tempting, attractive, and, yes, apparently so essential that we simply must get to the store or go online TODAY to make the purchase?

Tom Sine rightly makes parents squirm a little in this regard when he inquires and declares:

> What is the hidden curriculum in a Christian family in which the kids all have their own CD players, TVs, VCRs, phones, and when they get to a certain age, their own cars? ... [W]e are raising our Christian young people with a driven, acquisitive individualism that affects every facet of their lives, including the development of their sexual behaviour and their moral values. It is very difficult for the young to discipline their sexual appetites while living in an environment where their parents satisfy their consumer appetites with little discipline at all. (Sine, pp. 233–234)

It is neither logical nor fair to demand and expect our young people to go without in an area as powerful as their rapidly maturing sexuality, if we as parents refuse to control our material cravings and go without when it comes to caving in to society's insistence that we acquire all the latest goodies that modernity has to offer, ASAP!

A parent's influence is always powerful. We can shake our heads all we want at Rebekah's poor example as a tenured instructor of bold deception. The fact remains, nevertheless, that our ability to influence our children for better or worse is every bit as powerful. Whether that influence is explicit or implicit, our children catch on to the invalidity of our inconsistencies more quickly than we may even be aware.

So, Mom, Dad, when was the last time your kid(s) actually saw you "just say no?"

Chapter Seven: She's Good With Camels, Not So Good With Children

A mother's mistakes are never fatal to God's plans

Rebekah consciously taught Jacob how to excel at deceit and even had an innovative plan for every contingency. "But, Mom, Esau is so hairy!" Jacob hesitated, "Do you really think old, blind Dad is going to be fooled by our plan to deceive him into blessing me?"

Rebekah was already on it. "Not to worry, son. I have indeed thought of that." As a result of her creative conniving, Jacob lied to his father, invoked the name of God in committing the deceit and thereby expanded the rift with his brother, Esau, to the point where it became in Jacob's best interests to get out of Dodge.

By way of consequence for her award-worthy deceit, Rebekah ends up having to send Jacob away in order to save his life following Esau's pledge to kill little brother, once Isaac died. As if to add insult to injury, Rebekah steers Jacob to go spend some time under the nefarious influence of her brother, Laban, who similarly held an earned advanced degree in deception.

There is no clear indication in Genesis that Rebekah ever again saw the son she had so earnestly loved and so thoroughly corrupted. I therefore cannot help but wonder what memories may have haunted her as she grew old. Did she experience any remorse for how she had home-schooled Jacob? What regrets did she have in her later, lonely years? Did she perhaps live to encounter self-loathing for her blatant failures as a wife and mother? Did she ever consider herself a loser as a mother, like some women I know?

We are not given the answer to any of those questions in the text. Rebekah's years as a mother are left to decay like a foul aroma in the Genesis account. There is, sadly, very little in her record as a mother or wife that makes her a worthy example whom modern parents do well to name their daughters after. Maybe she opened a pet store in her senior years, I do not know. What is clear is that she definitely comes across as being far better with camels than with children.

It is instructive to note that whereas Rebekah's nurse merits mention in 35:8, Rebekah does not even receive the courtesy of an obituary from the author(s) of Genesis. At the end of her appearance in the text, we are left to conclude and somehow reconcile the fact that God, apparently, uses some very curious specimens of humanity whose glaring faults in character do not, however, prove fatal to his overall purposes.

Chapter Eight:
Just Call Me "Jake, the Snake"
(Genesis 27–35)

You've got to wonder what Jesus was like at seventeen. They don't even talk about it in the Bible, he was apparently so awful.
(Anne Lamott, 2007, p. 192)

In the last chapter I joked that Rebekah gave birth to the founding members of World Wrestling Entertainment (WWE). To take that comparison a step further, I will now make the suggestion that one of the twins, Jacob, may well have been the original professional wrestler named Jake the Snake.

During the 1990s when WWE was known as World Wrestling Federation (WWF), the multibillion-dollar entertainment empire owned by the Vince McMahon family featured a lanky, long haired wrestler designated Jake the Snake. A part of his belligerent character routine was that a good-sized canvas sack always accompanied him to the wrestling ring for his bouts.

In the late stages of each match when Jake the Snake was about to triumphantly subdue his opponent, a standard part of the choreographed dual called for Jake to disgorge the contents of the large bag that contained a live adult python which he would then deploy to further terrorize his panic-stricken victim.

Many centuries before anyone ever heard of the WWF star known as Jake the Snake, there was another wrestler deserving of that title: a man named Jacob whose story is related in the chapters of Genesis noted above.

Slippery? Jacob excelled at such. Crafty? He personified it. Devious? He majored in the art. A schemer? He was proficient at that skill as well. Jacob strikes me as the kind of guy who ate, drank and slept deception morning, noon and night. Consider his duplicitous record as uniquely summarized by Frederick Buechner:

> Twice he cheated his lame-brained brother, Esau, out of what was coming to him. At least once he took advantage of his old father Isaac's blindness and played him for a sucker. He out-did his double-crossing father-in-law, Laban, by conning him out of most of his livestock when Laban was looking the other way, by sneaking off with not only both the man's daughters but just about everything else that wasn't nailed down including his household gods. Jacob was never satisfied. He wanted the moon, and if he'd ever managed to bilk Heaven out of that, he would have been back the next morning for the stars to go with it. (Buechner, 1979, pp. 63–64)

So far in my musings in this book, I have identified the glaring shortcomings of such respected Biblical figures as Abraham, Sarah, Isaac and Rebekah. We have seen that certain aspects of their stories are not at all attractive. Sin usually leaves a fetid stench in its wake.

However!

Cue Bachman-Turner Overdrive again, because "B-b-b-baby, you ain't seen nothin' yet!" (Bachman-Turner Overdrive, 1974). Here comes Jacob and he spares no effort whatsoever to best them all when it comes to inappropriate behaviour, some of which we have already identified in the last chapter that covered the life of his mother.

With all the lying, manipulation and deceit we have already encountered in Genesis, readers could be excused for concluding we are reading a modern newspaper. "I thought the Bible was supposed to contain good news," someone might ask. "It does!" I respond. "How can you say that with what we have encountered so far in just the first book?" they retort. "You call this stuff good news?"

Yes, I do. But that is only because of a conscious choice I make as I read Genesis to continually keep my focus on God's grace. Genesis is proof that God's grace shines brightest against the backdrop of human disgrace. To cite Buechner again, this time with respect to the larger portrait we are to craft from the biographical disarray featured in these dramas:

> ...God doesn't love people because of who they are, but because of who he is. *It's on the house* is one way of saying it and *it's by grace* is another, just as it was by grace that Jacob of all people who became not only the father of the twelve tribes of Israel but the many times great grandfather of Jesus of Nazareth, and just as it is by grace that Jesus of Nazareth was born into this world at all." (Ibid., p. 65)

These stories are not chiefly a compilation of anecdotes from the lives of Abraham, Sarah and the others, then. Rather, they constitute a series of verbal photographs that convey a fundamental education concerning what Yahweh, the God of Genesis, is like at the core of his character—ever gracious.

Most of us do not need to be reminded concerning how depraved humankind is (although, as TMZ.com verifies, many are eager to profit from the sale and distribution of such). Disappointed and discouraged as we may become whenever we hear of moral failure on the part of leading religious figures, at such times we are better served to focus on what we should learn about the character of God via his unfailing commitment to those who fail.

What, then, does Jacob's sordid biography have to say to us regarding God's nature?

God is inexplicably gracious

By this simple statement, I wish to underscore yet again that God has forever displayed a disposition intent on dispensing unmerited favour our way for no reason other than his innate goodness. He persists in gracing us so that his own purposes prevail, fully aware that most of us will demonstrate in the process that we are self-serving scoundrels. Curiously, as previously noted, we seem to best catch glimpses of the brilliance of God's graciousness when it is held up against the darkness of mankind's affinity for offense.

From what we are told about Jacob in Genesis, it is not at all difficult for me to conclude that he was not the kind of person I would choose as a neighbour. Right from the opening verses that describe his character, he strikes me as the kind of guy who would steal carrots from your garden after dark. He would then casually mention over the fence the next day that although he did not know about you, as far as he was concerned, parents of neighbourhood hoodlums were allowing their brats to stay out far too late these days which accounted for the increase in theft and vandalism in the community.

And he would say this while looking you straight in the eye.

Jacob was the type of neighbour who would borrow your lawn-mower, use it to lay waste to the stubborn, wiry shoots from young saplings, then return it to you after the motor seized up saying, "I am really sorry, but thank the Lord we as believers have victory over any hard feelings that might arise when such mishaps occur, right?" And, if you were not a believer, he would return the ruined lawnmower with a copy of a pamphlet titled "*Jesus Will Save You From Hell*" attached.

The chances of Jacob winning the Good Neighbour Award were not likely although he would probably do all he could to become chairman of Neighbourhood Watch. He is the guy that has you muttering under your breath, "One of these days, someone is going to get you good and the sooner, the better, you loser."

The neighbour from hell, we might say, save that it was widely rumoured he was among those chosen by the God of the universe.

The scenarios that unfold in these chapters in Genesis should leave readers shaking our heads. Can you believe it? Jake the Snake has been forced to flee his neighbourhood because his own brother has threatened to kill him. En route to Uncle Laban's School of the Darker Arts to obtain an advanced degree in Con-Artistry, Jacob stops for the night and beds down under the stars. No sooner has he

Chapter Eight: Just Call Me "Jake, the Snake"

begun to slumber (28:10), than God appears accompanied by a few angels.

We are starting to rub our hands in anticipation because this is precisely what we have been waiting for—for Jacob to receive his just deserts. "You have met your match now, Jake," we are thinking, "time to answer a few questions about your deviant ways."

Let's listen in, then, as God tells off this prospective Mafia don:

> ...and the Lord said, "I am the Lord, the God of your Father Abraham and the God of Isaac. I will give you and your descendants the land on which you are lying. Your descendants will be like the dust of the earth, and you will spread out to the west and to the east, to the north and to the south. All people on earth will be blessed through you and your offspring. I am with you and will watch over you wherever you go, and I will bring you back to this land. I will not leave you until I have done what I have promised you. (28:13–15)

"Huh? Say what? Hello!? Would you say that again, please? I thought I heard God saying something to Jacob regarding Jacob blessing people and God watching over him. Surely, that cannot be! Jacob does not bless people; he abuses them! Jacob does not need God to watch over him; the people Jacob interacts with need God to watch over them, for heaven's sake!"

Any respectable reader has to do a double take here. This sounds far more like God telling Jacob to stay the course than the Almighty dispensing the chewing out that this jerk, uh, merits. Did I hear God say he would protect Jacob? No, no, no. God has got it all wrong; he is a busy guy after all, you know. Jacob is the dude people need to be protected *from* since he is actually the threat to the welfare of the community.

God says he is going to give Jacob everything? "Excuse me, Almighty One, but he is already well on his way to unethically obtaining everything there is to get as it is! He is doing quite well without your assistance, thank you very much."

"Some showdown, some confrontation, some rebuke this is. I want a refund on this show. The police lineup photo of this ne'er do well is on every post office wall in the country and, when God shows up, the first thing God talks about is protecting him? Really, God? In the name of all that is decent and fair, the least you might do is dole out some kind of censure and disrupt this con-game. At minimum, surely a good slap upside his head is warranted."

Seems not. Again, we are looking at what Jacob merits. God's favour is unmerited. There is nothing Jacob can do to make God love him more, and there is nothing Jacob can do to make God love him less. That is the plan God set in motion in the opening pages of Scripture. If we do not like it, we can perhaps take it up with him personally some day.

Instead, we are left to conclude that we have been watching too many *Lone Ranger* reruns or one too many *Rambo* or *Terminator* flicks. Hollywood teaches that, in time, the good guy always ends up tuning in the bad guy, right? So, what then is going on here? The good guy here isn't just any old good guy. Ostensibly, he is the only truly Good Guy. And yet all he has to say and do is talk about how much he is going to bless the bad guy. What's up with that?

God is gracious, period. God is gracious, regardless. God is gracious, come what may. God is gracious, discussion over. Enns and Byas instructively note:

> We might expect God to reprimand Jacob for being a little liar, as any parent would. Instead, he reiterates the promise to Abraham: Jacob's offspring will be uncountable and a blessing to all peoples of the earth … Given Israel's less than stellar history later on, an ancestor like Jacob *who still meets with God's approval despite his shortcomings* would be most reassuring. Jacob, like every one of his ancestors is a flawed hero. Screwing up is deep in Israel's genes;

God carrying them along regardless is deeper still."
(Enns & Byas, p. 86) (emphasis original)

It may be a good idea to pause and note the graphic importance of the ultimate storyline and how it is so creatively crafted into the narrative of Genesis. You see, the first book of the Bible could be filled with all kinds of theological declarations and elaborate explanations regarding what God is truly like. It could state with straight forward propositions that Yahweh is a God of grace, that his entire orientation towards us is to extend to us other than what we deserve (unmerited favour). Genesis might have laboriously explained that grace is the extension of a kind of divine philanthropy in response to human depravity, something far beyond what we can fully comprehend on a cognitive level.

But the divine Author does not do that. What he directs the human writer(s) to do is paint a few pictures, tell a few stories, share a few anecdotes including an ample amount that are not very pleasant at all. We are introduced to a succession of liars, cheaters, doubters, double-crossers, extortionists, et al.

And what is God's initial response to all of this?

He shows up to catch them in the very act and tell them: "Hey, just wanted to remind you that the original deal is still on. I am still planning to give you that land I promised, Abraham. I am going to make of you that great nation, Sarah. I still intend to protect and honour you, Jacob, despite the fact that you couldn't care less about protecting even your own kin."

Most of us have hesitations about grace being extended so freely, so nonchalantly, so lavishly. Unless we are the one in need of it.

How do we come to grasp what grace truly is and the kind of God that is its Ultimate Dispenser? We know what grace is when we see over and over and over and over again how self-serving, duplicitous and conniving mankind is, yet hear God say in essence: "Yep, those are my kids. Aren't they great? I have wonderful things in store for them. I am going to bless them. I sure do love them even though they couldn't merit my favour if they tried, the losers."

Engage with me in some candid reflection at this point. Be honest, we are kind of disappointed, aren't we? When God meets Jacob on that dark night, we want to see God rough him up a bit, grab him by the scruff of the neck and say, "just what do you think you are doing, you worthless scoundrel?"

When that does not happen, we want to say, "Really, God? How can you let this guy get away with what he has been doing to people time and time again? Do you not know that he goes to the local Baptist church and runs the risk of totally destroying the reputation of that congregation, not to mention your reputation also? What are people going to say when they find out that when you caught up with that master of me-first, you totally affirmed him, that you said nothing at all to reprimand or correct him for the error of his ways? What gives on that, God? Do you not comprehend that silence is tantamount to consent?"

We can well relate to Bill Moyers' and Burton L. Visotzky's candid contributions to the PBS panel discussion at this point:

> …[T]his is one of the most powerful and disturbing passages in the whole of the Hebrew Bible. Earlier God has been so angry at what people are doing on the earth that He decides to wipe them out and start over. He destroys Sodom and Gomorrah, innocent women and children, in His anger. This is a wrathful God of vengeance. Now, all of a sudden … God finds this duplicitous fellow on the run, who has cheated his family and continues to deceive, and God pats him on the back and says, "That's okay." Suddenly there's a mercy here that was not available to the innocent. (Moyers, (Ed.), p. 284)

> I think God exacerbates the problem. God is like parents who say, "Don't worry, sweetie pie. Whatever you do, I'll be here." And meanwhile the kid's standing there, having drawn on the wall. In a way, God makes Jacob worse and leads him to more duplicity…God essentially says, "You can behave

> however you want. I'm going to bless you, I'm going to protect you." God does this immediately after all the duplicitousness...the moral implications are very disturbing. That chosenness can in some way free you from moral obligation is a terrifying thought. In some way, it replicates what we saw with Abraham. Abraham does all kinds of things that are not quite on the up-and-up, and God rewards him. (Ibid., pp. 282–283)

Thank you to these gentlemen for articulating what most of us should be thinking or feeling. Jacob's performance is to be expected—he's human, after all. But God's? God's behaviour leaves us in a state of perplexity, our mind filled with questions.

When we focus solely on the behaviour of others, we choose to miss the inexplicable nature of the truth that our God is gracious. Until we put ourselves in the picture, that is. Genesis speaks to us of that reality over and over again as it is played out in the lives of people that we can relate to because they are just like us. I have no other explanation for the inexplicable than to assert yet again: we comprehend grace best (that which God is in his essence, that which comes naturally to him) when we see it against the dark backdrop of that which we are by nature.

Wow! It turns out that the loser I do not want as my neighbour and that I so desperately want to see meet his match, God meets alright. He meets him not to punch him in the face, but to pat him on the back and assure him that he would stay the hand of those who would attempt to pummel him. Puzzling as that may be, there is encouragement here for us.

Roberta Hestenes necessarily reminds all losers that God is inexplicably gracious.

> ...For me, it's very important that Jacob not be whitewashed, because if the hidden assumption here is that God should work only with people who are perfect, or that God is somehow immoral, then I'm doomed. All of us are out of it. But God doesn't

work only with perfect people. The fact that God works with this person, with all of his conflicting pushes and drives and struggles, is a sign of hope that God actually works with human beings. (Ibid., p. 286)

God is nobody's fool

It may be tempting at this point in the Jacob story, to take a breather and permit ourselves the pleasure of simply marinating in God's grace as if Jacob's story in Genesis concludes with God appearing to Jacob to affirm that the blessing is still a Go. And they all lived happily ever after, right?

Some readers, might wish to ask, "so that's it? This God is so gracious that he essentially condones evil and allows shysters to get off the hook without so much as even a modest rebuke?"

Jacob's story isn't finished yet. Not by a long shot. Prepare yourself for more surprises.

There is a sense in which the Jacob account actually proceeds from bad to worse indicating that Jacob doesn't detect so much as even a whisker of rebuke in God's appearance to him as he hits the road on the run from Esau. That's right. Jacob's deception continues; it has yet to hit its peak season.

What we have established so far in the Jacob narrative is that God's fundamental orientation or, to put it another way, where God is coming from in dealing with those who for good cause might be considered losers, is grace.

But just as the story of Jacob does not finish at this point, neither does the story of how God deals with losers. The story of Jacob's encounter with his uncle, Laban, as related in chapters 29–31 is evidence that God certainly has, among other traits, a great sense of humour. He is nobody's fool. Do not miss that reality.

Upon experiencing some degree of safety following a warm reception at Uncle Laban's place, Jacob becomes eager to acquire a wife. He thus works out an agreement with Laban to obtain the latter's youngest daughter, Rachel, in marriage. Jacob had been suitably impressed upon seeing Rachel's competence in working with animals. Perhaps it reminded him of the reports he had heard from his father, Isaac, or his mother, Rebekah, concerning her expertise with livestock.

Jacob agrees to work for Uncle Laban for seven years whereupon by way of compensation he was to receive Rachel as his bride. So smitten by Rachel was Jacob that seven years whizzed by seeming like only a few days before the time arrived for wedding bells to ring out.

The wedding gift from Jacob's prospective in-laws, however, was not at all what Jacob was expecting, I will forego the tempting invitation this scenario presents to employ some creative humour and simply state that, likely by careful use of the various customs of that culture, Laban succeeds in perpetrating a major deception against Jacob. After working for seven years as the bride price to obtain Rachel, Jacob wakes up the morning after the night before to find that he is actually married to the bridesmaid, Leah.

Enns and Byas again prove helpful in comprehending this romantic rhubarb:

> Maybe Jacob had too much of the wedding wine—or perhaps, as poetic justice, he inherited the blindness of his father. It seems that the trickster just got tricked. He should have known Laban was up to no good. It wasn't customary to marry off the younger daughter without getting rid of the older one first. But he didn't see that coming and so now he is stuck with Leah. At any rate, Jacob got a dose of his own medicine. He had earlier used Esau's urges to manipulate him out of his right as firstborn. Driven by his urges, Jacob is now tricked into giving the elder sibling what she deserved. Payback for what he did to Esau." (Enns & Byas, p. 87)

It is not surprising that Jacob immediately objects to being on the receiving end of deception this time around by demanding of Laban, "What sort of trick is this?" Ha.

Jacob was hardly a credible source to be giving anybody lectures concerning the evils of deception. The mix-up over the brides comes across as God's way of saying to this slow learner, "touché!" As if to rub Jacob's face in his lifelong record of trickery, Laban informs Jacob that whereas it may be somewhat of a surprise to a person of his ilk, in Laban's neck-of-the-woods, it was not to be overlooked that there were some definite advantages to being the first-born child.

Ouch! Boom! Esau…first-born…birthright…get it, Jacob? Who knows, maybe Uncle Laban was a Bachman-Turner Overdrive fan like Grandpa Abraham and proceeded to set his CD player to play *Gimme Your Money Please* (Bachman-Turner Overdrive, 1973).

Or perhaps Laban said like we might put it today, "welcome to reality, pal; what goes around, comes around." That which Jacob had so callously dished up to Esau in their youth, to his father in Isaac's old age, he now receives in return as a taste of his own medicine—a receipt for deceit.

There is no clear indication in the text as to whether Laban was consciously aware of Jacob's past record of deception which led him to carry out the Leah instead of Rachel stunt. Was he bound by local custom or was he merely acting out of the belligerence of his own depravity? What is clear is that, although Jacob agreed to Laban's terms to eventually receive Rachel in marriage, it came with the requirement that Jacob was to give Laban another seven years of labour. That's a significant amount of time for a master of a good scheme to plot revenge.

What is also evident is that Jacob's married life was fraught with the very same kind of domestic problems we have encountered before in Genesis: a barren wife, animosity between women related to fertility issues, a wife blaming her husband for her infertility, the introduction of maidservants to produce children for a wife, and so forth.

We can now breathe a bit of a sigh of relief. God is nobody's fool. There is finally a glimmer of God's justice shining through the dark clouds of deceit in the Jacob story. And it is difficult to keep a smirk from coming to your face, isn't it?

Same here.

God is remarkably tolerant

We have come to a place in the Jacob narrative where we are beginning to think: "Aha, take that, Jacob. You have so had it coming to you. Good for you, Laban. Bravo, God. Finally, a little bit of justice catches up with this con artist."

But Jacob is hardly yet finished with his uncle. His inventory of deception is nowhere near exhausted. He throws Laban another deceptive pitch and the story takes yet another almost predictable turn in terms of Jacob's bottomless bag of tricks. Jean-Pierre M. Ruiz appropriately wonders: "The story raises a very hard question: How can this kind of behaviour fit into the plan of God for a people?" (Moyers, (Ed.), p. 252).

We are not told whether any kind of reproach actually registered with Jacob as a result of the Leah for Rachel trickery carried out by Laban. Jacob eventually comes across as having merely been biding his time awaiting the right opportunity to get back at his uncle for the wedding that went awry as well as the various unfair labour practices Laban had been imposing on him over twenty years of service (31:41, 42).

As opposed to seeing in Laban's wedding day deceit any kind of justice or rebuke for his own penchant for treachery, in what amounts to proposing to Laban a most curious of agricultural-reproduction experiments, Jacob insists on receiving a kind of severance pay involving Laban's flocks. Difficult as the experiment is to completely comprehend from our cultural vantage point, the end result is that Jacob devises and effects another master plan of deceit with the result being that "the weak animals went to Laban and the strong ones to Jacob" (30:42).

Gotcha, Uncle Labe!

Putting his creative skills of deception to work yet again, Jacob essentially robs Laban of the very best of the latter's prized animals and promptly departs town without so much as the courtesy of leaving his forwarding address. When Laban finds out what Jacob has done, he pursues him likely with the intent of enforcing some kind of repayment or justice. God, meanwhile, intervenes and does not allow Laban to harm Jacob in any way. Once again, it is difficult not to feel some degree of perplexity as God seems to have minimal interest in Jacob being called to account for his devious ways.

What is particularly telling about what Jacob pulled off here is the response of Laban's sons in the early verses of chapter 31. There was no doubt in their minds at all that their cousin had not only outsmarted their father but had also cleaned out Laban's bank account in the process. By the time they had totalled up the net losses, their verdict was, "Jacob has taken everything our father owned and has gained all this wealth from what belonged to our father" (31:1).

Now, if you have not yet broken out in audible laughter over Jacob's remarkable skills at ripping people off, the text relates that not just once—but twice—Jacob observed that Uncle Laban's "attitude toward him was not what it had been" (31:2). Jacob whines to his wives, "I see that your father's attitude toward me is not what it was before" (31:5).

Uh, yeah! D'ya think, Jacob? And this surprises you?

There is no way I am giving this tidbit of hilarity a free pass. I have this recurring vision of Jacob saying to Laban, "Say, brother, have I done something to offend you?" To which Laban curtly responds: "Yes, you devious little bastard, you just blew up my retirement portfolio. My lawyers will be in touch."

Really, Jacob!

The scenario plays out, with yet another scene saturated in dishonesty when Jacob's wife, Rachel, steals her father's household gods. What is that all about for the wife of a guy whose name was about to be changed to Israel? His preferred wife doesn't share his faith? They hastily depart without advising Laban (31:19–21). When Daddy pursues, Rachel boldly lies to him about having her menstrual period so that her father could not locate the gods she had stolen from him (31:33–35). This head-scratcher of an account is then "resolved" by Jacob somehow getting Laban to agree that everything the former had stolen was truly deserved, whereupon some kind of a peace-covenant is contracted between them and they then go their separate ways.

I am once again indebted to Enns and Byas for the additional insight they bring to this gong show:

> These people are just a heartbeat away from the father of the twelve tribes and they are still dabbling with other gods! True, the prohibitions against idols and such are not given in the story until Mt. Sinai (in the book of Exodus). We could excuse their behavior as ignorance. But if Israel is shaping its story, as we've seen, why not leave out—or at least massage—the deceit, disbelief and idolatry? ... The answer, once again, is that the stories in Genesis mirror Israel's later history. The Israelites, from beginning to end, are not models of faithfulness to God and virtue. Yet, how does God react to all this? He does not overlook these misdeeds, as a clueless father might allow his children to run amuck in a restaurant. Rather, he disciplines his people and then presses on with the plan anyway, even with a less than stellar cast of characters. God looks past the inadequacies of his people to execute his plan to bring order back into a chaotic world ... God's unwavering faithfulness is summed up in a Hebrew word, *chesed* (CHEH-sed), which can also be understood as love ... It means that God is sticking

to his people no matter what. Again, this is not to condone bad behavior in Israel, but to draw attention to God's character: "This is the kind of God we worship, a God who is compassionate and faithful." You might even say that part of the reason Israel's story is told this way is to draw attention away from Israel and toward God. (Enns & Byas, pp. 88–89)

En route to a reunion with his estranged older brother, Esau, Jake the Snake one night has a curious wrestling match with a man who not only qualifies Jacob for a Handicap Only parking spot by injuring his hip, but advises him that his name will no longer be Jacob, but Israel. Jacob comes to recognize his assailant as God and once again, we are left with trying to somehow reconcile God's remarkable tolerance for Jacob's persistent deception as his chosen lifestyle.

Upon hearing that Esau is on his way to meet him (chapters 32–33), Jacob has a "come to Jesus" moment when he beseeches God for protection from Esau's expected settling of accounts between the two. He also prepares a significant gift of livestock as a peace offering to his older brother. When, to Jacob's surprise, Esau arrives on serene terms, Jacob realizes that he has found "favour" in his older brother's eyes (33:8–11) and suddenly becomes quite eloquent with respect to his understanding of the concepts of favour and grace! Nonetheless, he promptly returns Esau's kindness by lying to the older brother about meeting up with him later back toward their childhood home. He then proceeds to go somewhere else. The games of deceit continue for Jacob.

In chapter 34 via a story of a brutal massacre carried out by Jacob's sons in response to their sister being raped by Shechem, it is apparent that Jacob had successfully passed on his skills at deception to his offspring. By the end of chapter 34 we find this family in the midst of a major family fight with Jacob berating his sons "You have made me stink among all the people of this land!"

What? Jacob is now concerned about his reputation and wants to blame his own children for his being on the local police department's Most Wanted List? "Are you kidding me!? Since when did ethics and decency start meaning a hill of beans to you, Jacob?"

As for God's perspective on all this? Well, in chapter 35, in a rare moment of orthodoxy, Jacob advises his entourage that since they were getting close to where he grew up and there was a possibility they might encounter some people from his home church, his household best get rid of the foreign gods they were carrying with them. After all, you see, he fully intended to offer a sacrifice to Yahweh upon his return to Bethel.

And God? AND GOD? God affirms the change of Jacob's name to Israel, reaffirms his blessing on Jacob's line, and says in essence (35:11–12), "we need more of your type, Jacob. A nation and a community of nations will come from you, and kings will come from your body." I find consolation in Willimon's cleverly succinct reminder: "As we all know, our Savior is a sucker for lost causes" (Willimon, p. 177).

I am completely dumbfounded by God's graciousness. Actually, to be really honest, I am both baffled AND a little angry at God's graciousness. I am weary of trying to comprehend God's remarkable tolerance which at times in the story of Jacob comes across as his giving a free pass to Jacob to perpetuate his passion for deceit however and whenever Jacob deems it necessary.

You might again relate to this sentiment, however. I must once again confess that I seldom weary of God's remarkable tolerance when it comes to putting up with my unending string of misdeeds. I am actually very grateful when God directs his persistent grace my way.

Many people read the Old Testament and see only a God of brutality who not only tolerates but at times directly orders massacres and treachery. "What kind of God is that?" they derisively point out. Such questions are relevant and merit serious attention and careful thought. Nevertheless, when asking or attempting to answer such, it is imperative that the questioner engage the fact that the God of Genesis is consistently portrayed as a God of grace—inexplicably gracious, nobody's fool and remarkably tolerant.

Throughout Scripture, God is frequently referred to as the God of Abraham, Isaac and Jacob. That's because God has a grand sense of humour. Whenever people of that day and today hear(d) the names of these characters, the natural inclination is to roll our eyes and say, "Oh, yeah, those guys! Wasn't each of them a real piece of work! Those are your guys, God? You are their God? You certainly have quite the team of losers, there." We momentarily and easily forget that we are equally impaired.

God's willingness to be associated in any way with screwed up people like the rascals of Genesis says far more about him than it does about them. It also tells me that if there is room on God's team for Jake, the Snake and his busload of baggage, there may also just be room for you and me and the significant amount of personal detritus we lug around with us.

When I consider the story of Jacob through that lens, I find myself being far more grateful than grouchy toward God's spectacular patience with that shyster.

Chapter Nine: Out Come the Claws
(Genesis 29–35)

My friend Ethan says that being a parent means you go through life with the invisible muzzle of a gun held to your head. You may have the greatest joy you ever dreamed of, but you will never again draw an untroubled breath.
(Anne Lamott, 2007, p. 183)

Returning to a thread of thought that I introduced earlier in this book, I cannot help but wonder what their family reunions were like. Every family has its moments, to be sure. Yet as I read the account of Leah and Rachel, it quickly becomes obvious that Jacob's domestic life typified the proverbial dysfunctional family. The story reads like something right out of *Soap Opera Digest*.

What a plot line. Loan the basic details to novelist Danielle Steele and she would create a thriller to rival the sales of any one of her numerous best-sellers. Ms. Steele might even be able to create a screenplay based on the drama we see in the lives of Jacob, Leah, Rachel, Bilhah and Zilpah. Give it the title *Torn Between Four Lovers* and the ensuing movie would likely dwarf any version of *Fifty Shades of Grey* for Academy Award nominations.

What we have in this description is the kind of material you can find every day between 1 and 4 p.m. on network television. Scheming women and a man whose life appears to have been governed to a large extent by an insatiable libido.

In the last chapter we saw that things got off to a rocky start when Jacob's father-in-law, Laban, who was also his employer—oh, and his uncle—and the lady who turned out to be his first wife, Leah, who was also his cousin, cheated him so that Rachel the woman Jacob truly loved, who was also his cousin, had to settle for being wife #2, or cousin #2. It's complicated.

It did not help that Jacob took to making it obvious Rachel would also get more boxes of chocolates and bouquets of red roses than Leah come Valentine's Day simply because Jacob's love for Rachel was greater than his love for Leah. Ever noticed how women do not take kindly to having to share their husband's affections with another female, especially their sister?

Employing my twisted imagination, then, I can envision what a challenge it must have been for the children that were born as portrayed in this complicated story. Out feeding the camels one day, Reuben (Leah's firstborn) and Dan (Rachel's surrogate's firstborn) get into a war of heated words. Out of frustration one of them says—as kids are known to do—"my Dad can beat up your Dad!" To which the other replies, "My Dad is your Dad, stupid!"

"What? Oh! Right!"

Nor is it difficult, given what we see in this chronicle, for me to imagine Jacob as the president of the local chapters of HHA—Henpecked Husbands Anonymous. At one point, Rachel screams at him: "Give me children or I'll die!" To which Jacob might well have responded, "I have already given your sister four sons, so I don't think the problem in that regard is with me, sweetie pie."

From the perspective of twenty-first century North American culture, I am certain there had to be many times when Jacob found himself caught in the crossfire when the claws came out between his wives and the various mothers of his children. This is the kind of story that makes people say, "You couldn't write a script for that mess!"

Yes, you can. Are you still convinced popular TV shows like *Big Love* and *Sister Wives* can only originate in Hollywood?

In point of fact, this bizarre one, big, happy family is merely another of the many perspectives we are given in Genesis clearly establishing the truth that God is loser friendly.

Do you, like me, ever worry you have fallen short of God's ideal in some area of your life, that you have messed up so greatly that you are beyond forgiveness or redemption? Then gather in front of the spiritual mirror with the figures in this story and perhaps you will see that you are really not so bad after all. And, hey, they were part of God's original chosen people. There is likely some hope for you and me, then, from God's point of view.

There are numerous different approaches we could take in attempting to derive something of significance from this account. We could use the narrative to expound on the lack of discipline in the life of Jacob who seemed to have the typical male problem of keeping his pants up. But since I tackled some of Jacob's numerous faults in the preceding chapter, I will choose to be comparatively easy with him here.

I could wax eloquent on the female predisposition to cattiness and the frightful prospect of all four of the women in this tale simultaneously experiencing PMS. I could even offer some timely insights regarding why God in His wisdom deemed males to be the superior gender. But it is altogether too easy these days for enraged feminists—many of them members of my congregation—to Google my address for purposes of spray-painting my house or vehicle with graffiti startling in its graphic creativity as to what I might do with this book.

Further, since the Mrs. and I just celebrated our 41st wedding anniversary—which I think means I qualify for a couple of additional tax deductions or, at least, should—much as it pains me, I am going to refrain from dispensing additional insightful commentary on the rich topic of gender relations.

Rather, I will settle for a more politically correct take on this story in the interest of identifying that which hopefully has applicability to all of us in the course of, once again, engaging the marvellous reality that God is loser friendly.

When we choose to focus exclusively on difficult circumstances, there will always be ample cause for discontentment

If I could take a random sample of the people reading this book, I am confident it would be easy for every one of you to identify some circumstance(s) in your life at present that, should you choose to focus on it or them alone, could very easily render you chronically irritable and discouraged. That is the natural reality of being human in a world where we do not control much of what life sends our way.

Notice in the narrative regarding Leah and Rachel the strong sense of discontentment in which they are both immersed. Leah had plenty of children. And all of them were sons, a matter of significance in the culture of that day. She is portrayed, nonetheless, as a very dissatisfied woman owing to the fact that she was Number 2.0 on Jacob's list of favourite wives.

From chapter 29 one perceives that this lady's entire life revolved around her frustration at being rejected by Jacob. She names her first son, Reuben. It is a word that sounds like the Hebrew term for "distress" or "misery." (You thought you were the only person that had to carry your mother's emotional baggage around in your given name, didn't you? Not so).

"Uh-oh," you can just hear Reuben's boyhood friends saying, "here comes Misery!" Since, as the old expression claims, "misery loves company," it is not surprising that Leah gives her next son the name of Simeon which means "the Lord heard that I was unloved." Her self-esteem issues continue.

She names her third son, Levi, which essentially means "please love me!" By this time, Dr. Phil would likely have suggested to Jacob, "I think your wife is trying to tell you something, pal."

You get the picture, of course. Leah had plenty of children to give her love and affection, but that did not seem to be enough for her. It was as if she willingly looked past all the good things life

Chapter Nine: Out Come the Claws

was bringing her way choosing instead to focus on that which was proving to elude her.

I will refrain from being too harsh with Leah at this point because her view of life is a comparatively easy trap to fall into—focusing on what you do not have rather than on the numerous blessings you do possess. I have observed that it is a mindset that can ultimately lead to a lifestyle of relentless acquisition which can in turn lead to major financial debt which can then create excessive stress that, more often than not, we then assign to other causes. It quickly becomes a merry-go-round of misery so that people begin to consciously avoid being around you.

Had you asked her, Leah might have said she could not have been happier with her children. But, clearly, she appears to have wanted something more out of life. She seems to have lived her life in the emotional dumps because Jacob loved Rachel more than he loved Leah leading the latter to be governed by her anger at "that blankety-blank who stole my husband from me."

Be sure to not minimize Leah's plight. She had a right to her husband's love. But, hey, nobody ever said life was fair, did they? (I am frequently surprised by the number of believers I encounter who live with the notion that God or somebody in the Bible promised that life would be fair. No, Joel Osteen may have led you to adopt that conclusion, but it is not to be found in the Bible). We have choices to make every day as to whether we will focus on the blessings or the bummers that are inevitable parts of life.

As for the younger daughter, Rachel, 29:17 informs us she also had much that was going right for her. She was beautiful and, like her husband's grandmother, Sarah, may have even graced the covers of all the local fashion magazines. Perhaps Jacob treated her in accordance with what some people today call a "trophy wife." She likely kept pressing REPEAT whenever Eric Clapton's "My darling, you look wonderful tonight" played on the stereo.

However, good looks and her husband's kind attention do not seem to have been enough for Rachel. In 30:1 we find her screaming at Jacob: "Give me children, or I'll die!" Jacob responds, in essence, "Do I look like God?" and stomps out of the house to spend another day of frustration working on Uncle Laban's ranch.

So, despite what the billion dollar modern cosmetics industry daily advises, ladies, or regardless of what is insinuated by Madison Avenue entrepreneurs, it appears that even if you have the beauty of a Jennifer Garner or a Sandra Bullock, there is no guarantee you are going to be content with your life. Contentment can be very elusive.

Rachel learned that the implicit and explicit messages behind the articles written about her and the advertising contracts she had for the Revlons and L'Oréals of her day nonetheless left her unfulfilled. Again, female readers, note that a perfect figure (29:17) is not a certain ticket to satisfaction in life. Nor is a loving husband. Poor Rachel could not hit the clock-radio OFF button fast enough in the morning whenever the Beatles' *All You Need Is Love* began to play.

She wanted children, and she wanted them yesterday.

Pulling a page from Grandma Sarah's book on how to focus on the family, then, Rachel gives her servant Bilhah to Jacob to conceive children for her. As far as she was concerned, whereas she may have had the good looks and the enviable love, Leah kept elevating the competition and was winning the war concerning who was making the most trips to Baby Gap.

In case you think I am needlessly over exaggerating here, 30:8 states that when Bilhah gives birth to a son, Rachel names him Naphtali which means "I had a fight with my sister, but I am winning." I think that counts as an ancient form of our more modern "nah-nah-nah-nah-nah," doesn't it? These sisters are fully engaged in a tug of war to see who can win some kind of a contest that is never quite fully decipherable.

Regardless of whether you are female or male, do you see yourself in Leah and Rachel? Ripe with disillusionment, always focused on what you do not have in life to the point where your entire demeanour is freighted by discouragement and discontentment? Do you find yourself often convinced that what you have by way of material possessions, vocational achievements and a beautiful family is still not quite enough? Is your lack of self esteem owing to any number of numerous causes keeping you from enjoying life to the fullest? Do you frequently find yourself thinking "if only this" or "if only that" and truly believing that if only the "if onlys" would fall into place then the jigsaw puzzle for your contented world would come together on its own?

Both Leah and Rachel appear to have lived a good portion of their lives singing the "if only" blues. They did not seem to grasp that there will always be something we do not possess that someone else has, someone who performs some feat better than we do, someplace that we have not been where everyone else seems to have been. Like some of us, both of these gals needed to learn that when we focus solely on life's negative circumstances there will always be ample cause to be discontented and gripe that "life isn't fair."

When we consider God's constancy, we will always have ample cause for contentment

As I indicated at the start of this chapter, this is truly a remarkable story that yields numerous prompts for serious thought regarding such issues as contentment, self esteem, difficult relationships, parenting, marriage and so forth.

If you are in a meaningful relationship with a partner, imagine enrolling at your church or community association for a Relationship Enrichment Seminar. The featured speaker, after being introduced, arises and reads chapters 29 and 30 from the book of Genesis. He merely says, "I hope this story from God's Word will be a positive source of enrichment in your own relationships" before sitting down.

You would likely be among many who would respond, "What? That's it? I paid the full fee for a seminar merely to be read a story from ancient times about a couple of combative females? I want a refund."

But hold on a minute. Is there anything whatsoever of a positive or redemptive nature to be gleaned from simply an anecdotal overview of the lives of Leah and Rachel? Is there any relief offered in the text for the bitterness we can virtually taste as we read this tale of female rivalry? I am convinced there is and, hopefully, a competent relationship enrichment facilitator would be eager to draw such out for the benefit of registrants.

In 30:22, 23, Rachel's infertility eventually comes to an end when a son is born to her and Jacob that they name Joseph. Rachel exults that, at long last, God has removed her disgrace. Yet she is still not fully satisfied. She is looking for something more as evidenced by the fact that the name given the baby, Joseph, means "may he add" which for Rachel meant "May the Lord add to me another son."

I recall my mother trying to teach one of my nephews some basic dinner table etiquette when he was just learning to talk. At one mealtime, after she had passed him a plate of food without receiving any response, she inquired with the traditional instructive line: "What do you say?" Without missing a beat, he replied, "More, please." It is altogether too easy to live like that even as adults, I venture, always looking for "MORE, please" before taking time to fully appreciate what we already have.

Contentment was never a strong suit for either Leah or Rachel. However, if there is one story in Genesis that sparkles brighter than all the rest and brings about some kind of a hopeful ending to the chaos that is witnessed almost non-stop throughout the book, it is the record of Joseph's life (chapters 37–50).

Enns and Byas rightly point out that Joseph certainly had his own share of issues:

> Joseph, like most every other character we've encountered so far, starts off with some pretty serious character flaws, but turns out to be a key figure in

God's plan. At the outset, Joseph is a bootlicking daddy's boy. Israel even gave Joseph this beautiful robe, which he no doubt wore around his brothers, flaunting his favored status. The 17-year-old even tattles on his brothers. We hope the Genesis theme of sibling rivalry is ringing loud and true in your ears at this point—Cain and Abel, Jacob and Esau, now Joseph and his brothers. What gives? Israel's national history will be one big sibling rivalry event. The twelve brothers will in time become the twelve tribes of Israel, who will—wait for it—not get along. At all. The kingdom of Israel, unified under David and Solomon, will quickly split into two kingdoms, ten tribes making up the north and the remaining two (Judah and Benjamin) making up the south. Sibling rivalry is a civil war in miniature. (Enns & Byas, pp. 96–97)

The story of Rachel's son, Joseph, serves to efficiently underscore a couple of basic ground rules about the nature of God and how he interacts with losers in the course of bringing about his overarching plan. They help put a shine on an otherwise quite dismal story about two cantankerous and discontented ladies.

- a) Despite the seeming tragedies and inequities of life that we all inevitably encounter, take the risk of trusting that the invisible hand of a sovereign God is at work.

- b) God's ultimate blueprint is never stymied by the dysfunctionality of the losers necessary to help him bring it to fruition.

My younger brother, Phil, whom I referred to earlier in this book and his wife, Ramona, chose to name their daughter, Rachel. I do not know why, and I am not sure that I have ever even asked for an explanation, not that they owe me one. Nonetheless, it strikes me that perhaps I need to get on with the attendant lecture I previously mentioned that I sometimes offer errant parishioners in the course of gently upbraiding them for the myopia demonstrated in the naming of their children.

All kidding aside, allow it to register with you that there would not have been a Joseph without a Rachel. As becomes apparent in the Joseph narrative, God miraculously used Joseph to literally save Yahweh's chosen people from dying off when famine struck Canaan. It is another reminder to us that God is more than capable of using losers like Rachel and yes, you and me, to advance his eternal plan and accomplish good on his behalf.

And that brings to mind one thing I have remembered to tell my younger brother several times over the course of his attaining significant success as a popular Christian author/humourist. "You know, Phil, whether it be Abraham, Rebekah, Jacob, Rachel, or yes, yes Phil, even you, as the Biblical account of Balaam reminds us, God has been using jackasses for a long, long time now to accomplish his purposes."

Selah.

Chapter Ten:
Skeletons in the Family Closet
(Genesis 38)

When God is going to do something wonderful, He or She always starts with a hardship; when God is going to do something amazing, He or She starts with an impossibility.
(Anne Lamott, 2005, pp. 33–34)

During my last year of seminary in 1984, I conducted a major research project on the subject of sexual abuse in the evangelical church world. My sole motivation was that I desperately needed a topic directly related to a course I was taking in Family Counseling and the deadline for submitting my proposal was imminent. Bear in mind that this was in a time before the World Wide Web and prior to a period before stories regarding the horrors of sexual abuse among Catholic clergy became a staple in the daily news. The issue was not really even on the radar in North American society in general and certainly not with respect to the Church world in particular.

While scanning the *Chicago Tribune* one lazy, summer Sunday afternoon, I encountered an article about an incest trial wherein the accused was reportedly a respected leader in a local church. The writer indicated that people with knowledge in the field of sexual crime claimed that statistics regarding such incidents in religious circles were the same if not higher than they were in mainstream society.

In my naiveté, my immediate reaction was to dismiss the reporter's claim as but another example of what many perceive to be an established bias in media against religious beliefs and institutions. Upon further reflection, however, it occurred to me that I just might be able to leverage the topic into the academic project I so urgently needed to earn my degree.

One of the conclusions I soon reached as I trudged from one university library to another college library throughout metro Chicago was that, if indeed there was such a predicament in the Church community, nobody was talking about it. Nor had any one documented that they had studied the problem since I found only two or three brief articles in obscure academic journals that addressed the matter. Consequently, I ended up devising my own survey to distribute to whatever number at that time constituted a fair sample group of evangelical pastors across the American Mid-West.

I had no idea whatsoever regarding the unexplored snake's den I was probing with that academic stick.

Thirty-five years later, of course, it is almost impossible to believe that such a pristine world ever existed. The academy's recognition of the movie *Spotlight* at the February 2016 Academy Awards served as a shameful milestone marking the sickening reality of horrific secrets long covered up by numerous denominations, churches, missionary agencies and members of the clergy. (Recall the 2019 report involving the Southern Baptist Convention in this regard that I mentioned in Chapter Two). We now know with certainty that the troubling assertion I hoped to dismantle decades ago when I initially read that newspaper article is indeed fact and not fable. Psychologist Dianne Langberg reported in a July 2020 tweet that according to the American Medical Association about seven hundred thousand women are sexually assaulted each year in the United States. (Readers are encouraged to consult her urgently needed book *Redeeming Power: Understanding Authority and Abuse in the Church* available in the fall of 2020 (Brazos Press) for current statistics related to sexual abuse perpetrated in the religious sector).

The unsettling truth is that I should hardly have been surprised by or in denial about reports of sexual misconduct in religious circles. After all, such incidents show up very early in the Biblical narrative.

Grieved? Disgusted? Angry? Yes.

Surprised? No.

In subsequent years, I have been as active as possible in being an advocate for those who have suffered sexual abuse at the hands of perpetrators, similar to the father I read about in that initial newspaper article. Publicly professing Christian faith, many "perps" as we call them, are even employed by religious organizations as I reported in Chapter Two. I have come to deeply lament the automatic inclinations of too many religious organizations to immediately deny allegations of sexual crime in their midst and then spare no effort in attempting to cover-up and sweep such under the carpet. Religious leaders from the current Pope on down to the pastor of a tiny church in the hidden hollows of back country Kentucky need to do much better at reading the Bible they claim as their authoritative guide to daily life.

The writer(s) of Genesis were not surprised and made no effort at all to sweep hideous stories of gross immorality among God's people into a corner where no one would notice. The account of Judah and Tamar in Genesis 38 stands as an enduring exclamation point in this regard.

Most will agree that Genesis 38 does not make for pleasant reading. Thus, we make sure to skip that chapter in family devotions. And, no, the Sunday school teacher dare not consider reviewing that story with our children. What is it doing there, anyway, right in the middle of the emerging story of Joseph?

Oh, for sure, we all know about that verse in 1 Timothy 4:16 claiming that ALL Scripture is profitable, but surely, we can make some exceptions for the sake of public decency, can't we?

While serving as an associate pastor in a church, the lead pastor suggested one year that he and I preach through the book of Genesis together on alternating weekends and asked me to prepare the schedule for such an initiative. Without advising him, I went ahead and assigned him to preach Genesis 38 before slipping a copy of the schedule into his office file folder.

A day or two later he entered my office with an awkward expression on his face and said, "Uh, I see you have booked me to speak on that Judah and Tamar mess in Genesis 38." I acknowledged my conduct while doing my best to restrain a smirk from crossing my countenance. He then emphatically added, "I am not touching that! If you want to, be my guest!" I focused hard in order to keep from laughing out loud as I intoned in my best Baptist preacher's voice, "Brother, ALL Scripture is given by Go-wad and is prof-it-a-ble, is it not?"

The fun was just beginning. We had a tradition at that particular church where in the Sunday morning worship services one of the elders would read the Scripture that one of the pastors would preach from later in the hour. We had just welcomed a new, younger elder to the team and I noted in the week leading up to the Sunday I was to preach Genesis 38 that he was scheduled to read the Scripture that week.

I called him at his place of employment only to reach his voice mail. I decided to leave a brief message simply reminding him that he was in the cue to read Scripture that coming Sunday and advised him of the passage to be read. I then went on with my day.

That evening the telephone rang while our family was gathered around the dinner table. Seeing his number on Caller ID, I immediately answered. I did not get a chance to say much more than "Hell...," before a voice hollered at me over the line loud enough for the entire neighbourhood to hear, "I am NOT reading that!" I could hear the elder's wife laughing uproariously in the background. (May God bless you, Arnie, and give you and the Mrs. many more children in your old age).

In subsequent years I have related those incidents to numerous classes of budding preachers who have found great hilarity therein. Much of the content of this chapter comes from my accepting that challenge from my colleague back in the early 1990s to preach on

Genesis 38. Interestingly enough, and I will touch on this later, it was unquestionably the most appreciated sermon I have ever preached if I employ the standard of how many people booked an appointment to come to see me privately in the days and weeks afterward to talk about it. Most were relieved to finally be able to unload the emotional turmoil they had lived with for years because of some incident of sexual indiscretion that, usually through no choice of their own, had been forced upon them earlier in life.

Notwithstanding the somewhat embarrassing details of Genesis 38 and the discomfort such can provoke when publicly reviewed, the story presumably serves a significant purpose otherwise the writer(s) of Genesis would not have included it. In other words, just in case the message has not yet registered with us to this point in our review of the opening book of the Bible, let us be sure we get it now. Humankind has a persistent record with respect to the matter of being corrupt, of being sinful, of being losers. Call it what you want, it permeates into every area of life and the pattern of such behavior has been around a long, long time.

Sexual indiscretions among the people of God today are not, as some would want us to believe, indicative that we are living in the last days. I say that because the Biblical record makes it evident that they have been around since the earliest days.

Further, the story of Genesis 38 is one of several in the Old Testament indicating that sexual scandal by high profile religious figures did not begin with Rev. Jimmy Swaggart's notorious and well publicized fall from grace in the mid-1980s just as I was beginning my pastoral career. Not at all. For thousands of years now, a stunning declaration has tolled out from this chapter the startling yet healing truth that *the God of grace is not at all ashamed to identify with people of disgrace.*

I will cut to the chase in pursuing this theme by asking a relatively simple question: from which of the twelve tribes of Israel did Jesus Christ descend when he entered the world in human form?

God is Loser Friendly

Genesis 49:10 is the first of numerous Scripture references to indicate that when Jesus was born centuries later in Bethlehem, the Family Tree in the Family Bible in Joseph and Mary's home would have indicated that he was a descendant of the tribe of Judah. If that does not fully register with you, check out Matthew 1:1–16 where it is unquestionably clear that Jesus Christ was a direct descendant of Judah and Tamar and the twins born from this shameful union related in Genesis 38.

In noting yet again, therefore, the overarching truth being advanced in this book, that God is loser friendly, let us endeavour to derive something of usefulness from this eyebrow-raising anecdote about Judah and Tamar.

Jesus Christ knows what it is to be part of a family with skeletons in the closet

British newspapers recently carried an update on a sexual scandal that has troubled the modern Royal Family for several decades now. Shortly before the 21st-century arrived, it came to light that Captain Mark Phillips, the (now former) husband of Queen Elizabeth II's daughter, Princess Anne, had impregnated a New Zealand woman who then gave birth to their love child, a daughter named Felicity who is now 32 years old. The story resurfaced in the summer of 2017 when Felicity and her partner, Tristan Wade, who live in New Zealand, announced the birth of a son.

> This means that Felicity, who has just turned 32, is half-sister to Zara and Peter, the children of Phillips and Princess Anne, and that Felicity's first-born son James is now a 'secret' first cousin to Zara's three-year-old daughter Mia. Today, Zara, 36, is separated by 12,000 miles and a seemingly insurmountable social gulf from this latest addition to her family, who lives with his mother and British father Tristan in New Zealand. Yet they are connected by genetics, by appearance and even by a shared love of the

equine world. Felicity, herself a keen rider, is a specialist equine vet, and Tristan is an accomplished polo player, who only two years ago was playing in front of the Queen and Duke of Edinburgh at Windsor. (Oliver & D'Antal, 2017)

Current statistics indicate that many of us have a "Judah" or a "Captain Mark Phillips" in our family circle who has a history most are aware of although nobody wants to engage the matter. Most of us would really prefer not to be associated with such deviants, let alone related to one. It is always awkward when they show up at family reunions because everyone has to put on a false show of goodwill to these brothers, cousins and uncles whose presence invariably produces painful silences and anxious eye contact among the women.

Years of experience with victims of sexual abuse have taught me that many of you reading these words have such a person whose presence at family get-togethers strikes fear into your soul for reasons known only to you, them and God—or so you hope and pray. If that is your painful truth, may this historical fact speak comfort and peace to you regarding the compassion and understanding of God as they relate to the sordid truth you have lived with for too long. Jesus Christ was born into the family of Judah, a character who comes across in the text as little more than a dirty old man.

If such is a part of your experience, I plead with you to be aware that there are many gracious followers of Jesus who are willing to help you acknowledge the truth and seek emotional healing if sexual abuse of some variety has been or is a part of your life. I cannot urge you strongly enough to seek out such a trustworthy individual you can confide in regarding the horror that has burdened you with shame, guilt and remorse for too long now. Please know that regardless of what you might think or feel toward yourself, in all likelihood, you were not and are not to blame for what happened. There is no reason for you to continue to carry that burden. Should you wish, please be in contact with or "Google" me. I promise to confidentially put you in touch with someone in your geographical area who has the compassion, credibility and experience necessary for assisting you in dealing with the heinous wrong of sexual abuse (please see pp. 195–196 for selected recommended resources on the issue of sexual abuse in religious circles).

Judah and his family were second-to-none in terms of being a family of losers. For one thing, Judah himself embodied disobedience. He married a Canaanite woman in direct disobedience to the directives of God given his relatives as found in Genesis 24:34–38 and 28:6–9. One of his sons, Er, is so disobedient and wicked that God finally just ends his life. Another son, Onan, refuses to abide by a cultural practice which, regardless of whether we modern Westerners understand or approve, was the means for insuring that Er's widow would be loved and provided for throughout her remaining days. Onan wanted the pleasure of sex without any of the responsibilities entailed. How twenty-first century like does that sound? God therefore requires his life as well. Disobedience and self-centredness thrived in the genes of this family.

Deceit is another family trait that surfaces in this story. I think we have encountered that before in Genesis, right? In verse 11, Judah promises to give Tamar his third son as a husband, a promise he apparently had no intention of ever keeping. Knowing how shameful it was in that culture for a woman to be without a son to provide for her, Tamar plots a way to not only get even with her father-in-law for deceiving her, but devises a means to also become a mother. In so doing, she verifies the Scripture's assertion that "the heart is deceitful above all and desperately wicked" (Jeremiah 17:9).

And talk about a family with double standards. In verse 24 we find Judah self-righteously declaring that his daughter-in-law should be burned to death for prostitution, all the while knowing that he himself was just as guilty as she was. "Bring her out and burn her!" he fervently shouts. It is not unusual at all with respect

Chapter Ten: Skeletons in the Family Closet

to matters of sexual abuse for the initial blame to be placed on the innocent party who is usually a woman.

Judah's behaviour here is a good reason why we are well advised to be wary of those who make haste to vociferously condemn people caught in immorality. Someone might well have asked of Judah, "and what are you trying to hide?"

What a shameful family Jacob, the legendary deceiver, brought into being! And what a sordid reputation was established. Would you have wanted to be attached to his family name given the gossip that would have circulated on a regular basis?

Numerous people have confided in me as their pastor something along the lines of "You know, I never would have chosen to be born into the family I was." They have then gone on to share disturbing details of some aspect of sexual impropriety perpetrated on them years ago leading to long-term strained relationships that have proven a colossal burden for them to shoulder in life.

Some of you reading this have known what it is to be severely wronged by family members perhaps to the point where you have had to cut off ties with them in order to try and protect yourself and your own children all the while trying to reduce intense personal sorrow and recrimination. While families can indeed be the source of immense joy, they can also produce deep and lasting misery particularly with regard to inappropriate conduct of a sexual nature as we see here in the story of Judah.

Again, I plead with you, if this has been your experience and you have not as yet revealed such to anyone, recognize that Jesus can certainly relate to your experience in this regard. As I have rejoiced to witness over the past thirty-five years, he is raising up a wonderful team of people worldwide from whom you can secure appropriate counsel.

Jesus might have descended from the tribe of Gad, I suppose. We are not told much about that brother's line at all. It was not to be, however. God, in his astounding wisdom, mercy and favour, chose to have his son, Jesus Christ, descend from the motley crew that we see in the line of Judah, a family with skeletons in its closet. Such, I am convinced, is indicative of the strategic markings of the ultimate package of amazing grace that God sent into the world.

The willingness of Jesus Christ to be associated with disgraced people should challenge us with respect to our own attitude toward being associated with disgraced people

At one point in my pastoral career, I was asked to sit on our denomination's Discipline Review Committee. It was entrusted with making disciplinary recommendations regarding the credentials and careers of pastors who had succumbed to behaviour along the line of Judah's experience. During my tenure on that committee, we were called upon to process one situation regarding a pastoral colleague who several years prior had been convicted of child molestation allegations, a crime for which he had been incarcerated. He had now been released from prison and, for whatever reason(s), was seeking to again be approved for pastoral ministry.

Understandably, many people find such stories repulsive and would even suggest that the credentials of such a person should never be restored to enable them to once again be a leader in Christian ministry. There is wisdom in such a perspective. Accordingly, the members of the team I was a part of on that particular case reflected a diversity of viewpoints as to the appropriate action that should be taken. Numerous factors were discussed at length and at times the debate reflected strong emotions as we sought to determine what solution we would implement and what our rationale would be for such.

In the course of our discussion, I suggested to the committee that one of the factors I believed we needed to consider in the matter required us to ask the question: what does the fact that God is loser friendly mean in this particular scenario? On the other hand, of course, to what extent should a solution reflecting a zero-tolerance stance that is appropriately common today in the thinking of some

Chapter Ten: Skeletons in the Family Closet

be permitted to prevail in such a case? Some members of the committee were annoyed—even angry—at me for registering the perspective that I did regarding the loser friendly God.

I gently and patiently tried to explain that if, as believers proclaim so emphatically, the heart of the Christian gospel is the distinctive message of redemption, reconciliation and second chances, what bearing did that reality have on the decision we were being asked to make that day? There are many difficult questions that confront us when it comes to determining what the application of grace looks like in daily life concerning the heinous behaviours that God's people are capable of perpetrating. Given what I see regarding God's extension of grace in the book of Genesis, I am compelled to ask: how are we doing at walking grace as opposed to merely talking grace?

Another way to articulate the issue is to ask: what does grace look like when applauded and applied in the muck and mire of everyday life? At a minimum, as it relates to the story of Tamar and Judah, I am insistent the fact that Jesus Christ was linked to disgraced people both in his own family's history and in the way he conducted himself on earth must be reflected by those of us who call ourselves by his name. Short of that, we may have a religion, but we do not have a genuine message of redemption that, we maintain, is what broken people—which all of us have been, are or will be—need most of all.

Why do we take the stances we do in situations where grace is needed? Why do we not take a stance that we might take at such times? Why does it always seem we find it comparatively easy to apply the sentiments found in the grand old hymn *Amazing Grace* to ourselves but not to the other guy? Sometimes when I listen to those who claim to be recipients of the grace of God speak about those who have fallen into disgrace, I am inclined to think we would actually be more authentic if we amended the words of the hymn to "Amazing Grace, how sweet the sound; that saved a wretch like me (but not you)."

If there is one thing that stories like this regarding Judah and Tamar should teach us, therefore, it is that God may not be as favourable toward cataloguing or categorizing sins the way we so often do as believers. In Alberta, Canada, where I live, the beef industry regularly advertises certain cuts of steak as "Grade A, Canada #1 choice, sirloin," a measurement of quality that I have referred to earlier in this work.

I am of the opinion that this is the approach many in the Christian church take with regard to how we view sin. Murder, adultery, homosexuality, abortion—obviously those are superior evils, or Grade A, Canada #1 wrongs. On the other hand, gluttony, materialism, gossip, greed, misguided priorities—those practices or habits that I am conspicuously guilty of—well, for whatever curious reason(s), they are much less offensive to others and, presumably, to God as well, right?

It can be a probing exercise, spiritually speaking, to ponder how we usually perceive ourselves to be not quite as bad a sinner as that person across the street. Or that woman seated across the church auditorium from us. Or that hopeless case we have to face in the office where we work.

Yet as I noted in an earlier chapter, I Corinthians 6:9 does not support living with that attitude. In St. Paul's view, all sins basically fall into the one category of, well, sin, and are apparently egregious enough to keep us all separated from God. If we are all the same in that one regard, sinners, then it seems to make sense that we have a common need for the only energy capable of lifting us out of the category of sinner—God's grace, his unmerited favour.

That was Paul's perspective because it was essentially the perspective of his Master. In Mark 7:20 Jesus identified greed, wickedness, theft, deceit, envy, pride, foolishness right along with sexual immorality and murder as ills that all proceed from the human heart. I can relate to some of these evils by personal experience, but not others. Nonetheless, it appears that Jesus places me in the very same category as the one who can experientially relate to those that I cannot—a sinner, in need of that which everyone else in that condition needs—grace. That means that in God's view I am as much of a sinner as any sexual abuser. It may not be a popular way to look at such matters, but bear in mind, "it's not about you" or your likes or dislikes.

The willingness of Jesus Christ to associate with disgraced people like his human ancestor Judah, or like you and me, is a beacon of hope that pierces the darkness of our own making. It summons those who identify by his name to replicate the attitude and actions of he whom we call "Lord" with a corresponding readiness to associate with disgraced people.

And that includes seeking the necessary help to come to a place of extending grace even to those "Uncle Judahs" who may have harmed us very, very deeply.

****

He'll Dry the Tears

He'll dry the tears from your eyes; He'll take the pain from your heart

He'll move the clouds from your skies; He'll dry the tears from your eyes

He knows the way that you feel; He's felt the weight that you bear

He knows it's all very real

For He is touched with the feelings of our weaknesses; He has been there too

In your despair, remember all his promises; He will see you through

He'll never leave you alone; He'll always stay by your side

A friend like none you have known; He'll never leave you alone"

For He is touched with the feelings of our weaknesses; He has been there too

In your despair remember all his promises; He will see you through

(Dallas Holm, 1986)

Chapter Eleven:
Celebrating a Reckless Grace

*Grace means you're in a different universe from
where you had been stuck; when you had
absolutely no way to get there on your own.*
(Anne Lamott, 2005, pp. 54–55)

If you have (re-)read the stories from Genesis that I have touched on in in this collection of essays in keeping with the presuppositions that I encouraged readers to employ in Chapter Two, you will be better able to appreciate my claim that God's goodness to humankind in the first book of the Bible is presented to we losers as a reckless grace.

I use the word 'reckless' intentionally while acknowledging the term may be uncomfortable for some of you. I recognize that the dictionary defines the term as "marked by a lack of thought about danger or other possible undesirable consequences." I am also well aware that some of its synonyms may not be initially perceived as very orthodox when used with reference to God: careless, irresponsible, out of control, *et cetera*.

However, I urge you to summon your best effort to consider the term 'reckless' from this perspective. In Genesis we see God's grace consistently bestowed on the kind of people who, from what we are told regarding their integrity or, better, the lack thereof, might very well have turned around and used or exploited God's unmerited favour to keep right on being the self-centered narcissists they had already proven themselves to be.

Is that not so?

Such was a risk that God repeatedly insisted on taking with the ancients, however. We saw as much in certain stories where we were flabbergasted, if not downright annoyed, at how God seemed to look past, indeed overlook altogether, wrongdoing. It is a risk, I contend, that he remains willing to take with you and me. If that strikes you as a recipe for eager abuse by humanity, be reminded that God has likely considered that possibility. Nevertheless, to my knowledge, he has never relented his willingness to assume that risk.

It is a gift of God that I have heard referred to as "extreme grace." I choose to label it a reckless grace. And, for God's repeated extension of it to this loser, I am most grateful. Whatever we choose to label it, it is the polar opposite of the "cheap grace" so appropriately vilified by Dietrich Bonhoeffer.

The reason God could and can continue to afford taking such risks, the explanation as to why he can continue to dispense reckless grace, was determined from before the foundations of the world. It is perhaps best expressed by the prophet Isaiah who declared concerning The Suffering Servant, "the Lord has laid on him the iniquity of us all" (Isaiah 53:6).

The various characters whose public failings are so graphically portrayed in Genesis, therefore, are presented to us as selected objects of God's grace whose sins God had predetermined would be covered by virtue of what was laid on Jesus Christ when the latter eventually died on the cross of Calvary. It is for this reason and this reason alone that God is justified in extending unmerited favour to the undeserving even to the point where, as we have repeatedly seen in Genesis, they appear to fail with impunity. Recall Rick Warren's sentiment that I began with: *It's not about them, or you, or me!* We, like they, can fail without seeming recrimination because we are blanketed by a reckless grace. It is actually not reckless at all, then, because such grace presupposes the death of Jesus as that which makes it the legitimate entity it is.

Abraham, Sarah, Sodom and Gomorrah, Isaac, Rebekah, Jacob, Rachel, Leah and Judah were all viewed by God through the lens of his plan for Jesus to come and engage in a showdown with the sins

Chapter Eleven: Celebrating a Reckless Grace

of the world. On this basis alone can the undeserving be treated as deserving. Only in this way can the sinful be viewed as sinless. Only in such a marvellous sphere of relationship between God and humankind can Philip Yancey's claim be validated that there is nothing we can do to make God love us more and nothing we can do to make God love us less.

The ideas and thoughts I have tried to communicate in this book will have been nothing but more interesting sentiment unless each reader who is a Christ-follower intentionally commits to this element of follow-through. Ask yourself right now as to what extent you are willing to be similarly reckless in the extension of grace to people in your world who deserve anything but grace. And then, look for the earliest opportunity to extend that reckless grace to them.

I mentioned at the beginning of this book that I was raised in the ethos of fundagelical Christianity. Those of you who come from a similar background will know that such an environment often had its definite shortcomings with respect to practical demonstrations of grace. Although the term was frequently heard and discussed, any exhibitions of the reckless grace displayed in Genesis were comparatively infrequent.

Due in part to my upbringing but even more so because of what I have witnessed in my own experience as a pastor and participant in the North American religious scene for the past thirty-plus years, I have committed to doing all that I can with the time I have left to being an unapologetic and indiscriminating distributor or conduit of reckless grace.

Let me hasten to affirm that it is a most demanding challenge that I have taken on and I fear there are many days when I fail abysmally at achieving my objectives. I too struggle with the reality that I remain more like Jacob than I care to admit. Since I claim, however, to be a beneficiary of God's reckless grace, the most appropriate response I can make to the Giver of such grace is to work diligently to honour him by selflessly endeavouring to pay it forward to others in need of a similar grace. The extent to which I am willing to be reckless in undertaking that task is the most accurate indicator I know of by which to measure the depth of my own experience of God's grace,

Several years ago, I had to do something that is altogether too common in church life these days. I faced a situation where I made a decision to terminate the employment of a colleague and a friend following my learning of an inappropriate conversation he had initiated with a female congregant. For various reasons, it was one of the most difficult decisions I have ever had to make as a pastor. And, to clarify, let me stress that by calling for a radical dissemination of a reckless grace, I in no way intend to convey that the consequences of wrongdoing by anyone should therefore be ignored or minimized. Again, to do so would violate Bonhoeffer's iconic and ever relevant denunciation of "cheap grace."

Following the elapse of a significant period of time following my decision to discipline my colleague by terminating his employment, an opportunity arose for this individual to return to our fellowship in a one-time support role for a ministry he was then assisting. Although I knew there would be opposition from certain powerbrokers in the congregation who had their own good reasons for their perspectives, I opted to allow him to return and participate in the worship service in question.

Predictably, some of the flock were dismayed and didn't hesitate to advise me of their frame of mind. Some, in fact, did not even attend worship that weekend as a means to visibly communicate and quantify their displeasure with my decision.

I accepted that when it occurred and still accept their decisions years later. They were and are fully entitled to their viewpoints and I try not to think any less of them for the positions they held.

I did what I did on that occasion because it is what I had to do. You see, when all is said and done in my life, the one thing I will not regret being faulted for at all is the accusation that I was too

Chapter Eleven: Celebrating a Reckless Grace

reckless in reflecting, sharing and demonstrating the reckless grace of God as it is revealed beginning in the pages of Genesis.

Just in case you have missed noticing the trend, our world is in urgent need of reckless grace for which I am advocating. Hurting leaders and congregations in the Christian Church desperately require it whether or not they recognize the fact. I am resolutely convinced it is the only reason for hope in days that, at times, seem hopeless in the Church world.

As I conclude, therefore, I sincerely ask you: if reckless grace is not to be found among the people who call ourselves beneficiaries of a loser friendly God, where exactly is it to be located and obtained in this world?

****

> Sweet, sweet grace of God! ... How shall I praise God sufficiently for the inexplicable miracle of divine grace in my soul-and how to explain it to others? ... Blessed in the meeting tonight with the force of the simplicity of it all and more than ever with the grace of the "happy God" who has thus opened his heart to man!

> I see clearly now that anything-whatever it is-if it be not on the principle of grace, it is not of God. Here shall be my plea in weakness; here shall be my boldness in prayer; here shall be my deliverance in temptation; at last, here shall be my translation. Not of grace? Then not of God. And here, O Lord Most High, shall be Your glory and the honor of Your Son. And the awakening for which I have asked, it shall come in Thy time on this principle by grace, through faith. Perfect my faith then, Lord, that I may learn to trust only in divine grace... (Elliot, (Ed)., pp. 178, 183)

Epilogue

Having written what I have in this volume, I hasten to affirm that my musings here reflect the inevitable idealism, altruism and room-for-improvement necessarily incumbent to any effort to apply divine concepts to the realities of the human condition. That is an appropriately veiled attempt to register my keen awareness that I have miles-to-go in order to better practically understand, more competently articulate and consciously improve my personal exemplification of the core ideas contained in this book.

To be pointed, I do not find it easy to extend grace either to myself or to others. Stated another way, I experience a sinister delight in helping the undeserving truly appreciate their shortcomings. Why is this? At the risk of committing some kind of theological or psychological offense to someone reading these words, I submit that part of my bent in this regard is owing to the fact that I was born a sinner and come from a long line of those similarly birthed with a significant amount of spiritual destitution. That is: my paternal and maternal relatives were heathen. British Baptist and Scottish Presbyterian heathen, to be sure, but heathen nonetheless. Regular social media interactions with my cousins on the other side of the continent regularly confirm that such is our enduring family heirloom. Seriously, think about it. I was born this way; what's your excuse?

I suspect another component of my being behaviourally challenged when it comes to granting grace also has to do with some of the attitudes and behaviours I absorbed while growing up in fundagelical circles. I think it is the Roman Catholics who reportedly claim something to the effect that if they are permitted to be the sole influence in a child's life for the first six or seven years, it doesn't really matter what additional factors come to bear on the youngster's life while growing to adulthood. The core values guiding their thinking and behaviour will have been successfully instilled for the duration of that person's life. I suspect there is a certain amount of accuracy to this equation which continues to also play out in my life. My two children with graduate training in Clinical Psychology affirm there may be something to be said for this argument although they demur to give serious reflection to the personal implications of them having been raised under my gaze.

Additionally, and possibly the single greatest factor affecting my skirmish with conferring grace on the undeserving, has been that I have been involved in a vocation for more than forty years now that requires I be somewhat adept at practicing what I preach when it comes to demonstrating grace to my congregants. Should you be unaware, let me clue you in to my studied conclusion that everyone in the Church world assumes they are an expert when it comes to matters theological and religious. Regardless of whatever minor doctrinal disagreements exist among those who profess faith in Christ, if you affirm the basic Christian belief that the Holy Spirit resides within the life of a believer, it is helpful for lay people to be aware that pastors hear all manner of claims being made within parish confines from those who launch a proposed settlement to any matter of disagreement by saying, in essence, "the Holy Spirit has shown me that...." What this should be interpreted to mean is that they are telling you "it does not matter how many degrees you have behind your name, Pastor. God has told me you are wrong and I am right when it comes to XYZ matter."

Readers should be aware that, lest I immediately be punted from their premises, I try not to follow this mode of behavior when I take my car to the mechanic or when I periodically visit my medical doctor. They would promptly tell me to "get lost." But we pastors are, um, too gracious—or, at least, expected to be gracious enough to withstand that which insults our professional training and decades of experience. Therefore, we—or I will speak only for myself here, I end up suppressing the inclination to laughter or controlled outrage at the expressed nonsense and opt to assume the role of Mr. Nice Guy. I've had to learn some hard truths about the boomerang psychological effects of the propensity to always present the pleasant persona.

Accordingly, I leave you with the reminder that even those of us who are trained and paid to discern and articulate enduring spiritual truth have our fair share of challenges when it comes to mastering what we mine or practicing what we preach. I continue to work diligently on my challenges and thank you for your patience in thinking with me through these pages along the intriguing and enduring vein of thought that GOD IS, INDEED, LOSER FRIENDLY.

Tim W. Callaway
Calgary, Alberta, Canada
Autumn 2020

Acknowledgements

When it requires almost 25 years to get a book from an original concept to the commercial shelf, it is apparent that the author could use some help. I am therefore necessarily grateful to many people, including some not named here, who have, without even knowing it, said something along the way that has prompted me to keep returning to a manuscript that I had laid aside yet just kept gnawing away at my mind and heart. Thank you! God knows who you are, and I pray affirmation and blessing on you all for your influence and giftedness. My specific indebtedness is due:

- numerous church staff & pastoral associates over the years: Myrna Koch deFehr, (the late) Tony Hanson, Doug Pippus, Tammy Virr, Cathy Peachey Irwin, Heather McKeeman, Brian Burkhart, Bob Bahr, Shane Bassen, Marlene Nordstrom, Linda Andreasen, Mark Bezanson, Dr. Bryan Clarke, Gord Klassen, Gary Hellard, Don Somerville, Shawn Anderson, Sindy Jeske, Jennifer Caspell, Lynn Michaels, Harold Amstutz, Dan Hardock, (the late) Rory Davidson, and Zach Wagenvoort; both Denise Daniel and Trish Kotow merit my particular gratitude for their help in tirelessly and capably organizing and formatting this manuscript

- personal & professional friends near and far: Rev. Mike and Kay Anderson; Dr. Paul and Lila Balisky; Terry and Marcie Balisky; Dr. Randall Balmer; Rev. Dr. William H. Barber II; Rev. Doug Barrie; Dr. David Batstone; Steve Baughman; Dr. Reg Bibby; Bryan Butler; Greg and Kristal Chalmers; John and Charlotte Cousley; Dr. Ron Galloway; Chuck and Karen Girard; Dr. Irving J. Hexham, Dr. Jeremy Hexham; Dallas and Linda

Holm; Mark Imbach; Rev. Mike Jones; Dr. Walter C. Kaiser, Jr.; Dr. Chang-han Kim; 'ede Klinger; Rev. Doug Koop; Trish Kotow; Dr. Glenn Kowalsky; Mark Kowalsky; (the late) David Kuo; (the late) Gordon Legge; Donnie McAreavy; Candis McLean; Janice Vert Baker Meeks; Dr. Gordon and Willa Meyers; Brenda Boytim Morrison; Bob and Joan Neufeld; John B. Pace; (the late) Rev. Harold Peters; Rev. Lloyd and Eileen Peters; Dr. Karla Poewe; Hal and Joan Rainforth; Stephen J. Rendall; Dr. Ted S. Rendall; Dr. John G. Stackhouse; Cliff Storvold; Boz Tchividjian; Joan Thomas; (the late) Ted and (the late) Bernice Vander Veen; Rev. Jim Wallis; Rev. Michael Ward; Dr. G. Douglas Watson; Inspector Bill Webb (ret.); Dr. William Willimon; Rev. John Wiseman; Paul Workentine; William Paul Young; Rev. Brian Zahnd

- our three children (and partners) who buoy me more than they will ever know with their love and their scholarly/vocational pursuits: Travis (MBA Durham, employed in the world of finance) and Mabel; Dallas (PhD studies in progress at Oxford) and Jennifer; Karis (PhD Western Michigan, now teaching Clinical Psych at University of Manitoba and also a PTSD therapist)

- Joyce Elaine (RN, OHN), my wife of 41 years (our kids have their Mother's brains and my credit cards!), who has stuck with this loser through ups and downs, successes and failures, thick and thin, student poverty and elusive wealth—essentially that "for better, for worse" ethic that some people today may still be familiar with

- and last but by no means least, my faithful canine companions who were alongside throughout—snoozing, distracting, editing, refining: Belle, Chubb, Molly, Mika and Bellah! Dogs are people too!

Bibliography

Blog posts:

Baughman, Steve. (2019). RaviWatch: Investigating the false claims of evangelist Ravi Zacharias. [Web log post]. Retrieved from http://www.raviwatch.com

Bedell, James. (2019). Willow-Gate: The Cover-Up. [Web log post]. Retrieved from https://drj1952.com/2019/08/04/willow-gate-cover-up/

McAlpine, Stephen. (n.d.). Different Mega-Church: Same Old Scandal. [Web log post]. Retrieved from https://stephenmcalpine.com/why-the-exposure-of-mega-church-scandals-follows-a-particular-pattern/amp/?__twitter_impression=true

Misek, Joe. (2018). Harvest Bible Chapel, Julie Roys' Report, and how to tell if you are in a church or an empire. [Web log post]. Retrieved from https://www.walkingwithalimp.net/2018/12/15/harvest-bible-chapel-julie-roys-report-and-how-to-tell-if-you-are-in-a-church-or-an-empire

Ortberg, John. (2018). Observations on the Chicago Tribune article re: Willow Creek Leadership. [Web log post]. Retrieved from http://www.johnortberg.com/observations-on-the-chicago-tribune-article-re-willow-creek-leadership/

Rauser, Randal. (2018). Ravi Zacharias: Apologist or Fabulist? An interview with Steve Baughman. Retrieved from https://randalrauser.com/2018/09/ravi-zacharias-apologist-or-fabulist-an-interview-with-steve-baughman/

Rauser, Randal. (2020, September 8). New Allegations that Ravi Zacharias engaged in Sexually Predatory Behaviour. Retrieve from https://randalrauser.com/2020/09/new-allegations-that-ravi-zacharias-engaged-in-sexually-predatory-behavior/

Rauser, Randal. (2020, September 13). The Ravi Zacharias Sex Scandal: A New Personal Statement. Retrieved from https://

randalrauser.com/2020/09/the-ravi-zacharias-sex-scandal-a-new-personal-statement/

Seitzinger, Tina. (2011). 52 Job Titles a Mom Holds. [Web log post]. Retrieved from http://www.lifewithoutpink.com/2011/05/16/52-jobs-titles-a-mom-holds/

Speight, Rob. (2019). A Deep Divide Remains at Willow Creek. How Come? Retrieved from https://robsp82.com/2019/07/

<u>Books:</u>

Anderson, David Robert. (2013). *Losing Your Faith, Finding Your Soul*. New York, NY: Convergent Books.

Armstrong, Karen. (1996). *In the Beginning*. New York, NY: Ballantine.

Balmer, Randall. (2006). *Thy Kingdom Come (An Evangelical's Lament): How the Religious Right Distorts the Faith and Threatens America*. New York, NY: Basic Books.

Barnhouse, Donald Grey. (1973) *Genesis: A Devotional Exposition (Vols. 1&2)*. Grand Rapids, MI: Zondervan.

Baughman, Steve. (2018). *Cover-Up in the Kingdom: Phone Sex, Lies, and God's Great Apologist, Ravi Zacharias*. Pennsauken, NJ: BookBaby.

Bly. Robert. (1997). *The Sibling Society: An Impassioned Call for the Rediscovery of Adulthood*. New York, NY: Vintage.

Bonhoeffer, Dietrich. (1963). *The Cost of Discipleship*. New York, NY: MacMillan.

Buechner, Frederick. (1979). *Peculiar Treasures: A Biblical Who's Who*. San Francisco, CA: HarperSanFrancisco.

Buechner, Frederick. (2006). *Secrets in the Dark: A Life in Sermons*. New York, NY: HarperOne.

Buechner, Frederick. (1988). *Whistling in the Dark: An ABC Theologized*. San Francisco, NY: Harper & Row.

Callaway, Phil. (2002). *I Used to Have Answers, Now I Have Kids*. Eugene, OR: Harvest House.

Callaway, Tim W. (2013). *Training Disciplined Soldiers for Christ*. Bloomington, IN: WestBow Press.

Elliot, Elisabeth (Ed). (1978). *The Journals of Jim Elliot*. Old Tappan, NJ: Fleming H. Revell Company.

Enns, Peter and Byas, Jared. (2012). *Genesis for Normal People*. Englewood, CO: Patheos Press.

Feiler, Bruce. (2002). *Abraham: A Journey to the Heart of Three Faiths*. New York, NY: William Morrow/HarperCollins.

Hamilton, Victor P. (1990). *The Book of Genesis: Chapters 1–17*. Grand Rapids, MI: Eerdmans.

Hinten, Marvin. (1983). *God is Not a Vending Machine: So Why Do We* Pray *Like He Is?* Grand Rapids, MI; Zondervan.

Kaiser, Walter C., Jr., (1983). *Toward Old Testament Ethics*. Grand Rapids, MI: Zondervan.

Klein, Naomi. (2000). *No Logo: Taking Aim at the Brand Bullies*. Toronto, Canada: Knopf.

Lamott, Anne. (2007). *Grace Eventually: Thoughts on Faith*. New York, NY: Riverhead Books.

Lamott, Anne. (2005). *Plan B: Further Thoughts on Faith*. New York, NY: Riverhead Books.

Lamott, Anne. (2013). *Stitches: A Handbook on Meaning, Hope and Repair*. New York, NY: Riverhead Books.

Moyers, Bill. (1996). *Genesis: A Living Conversation* (Companion to the public television series). New York, NY: Doubleday.

Noll, Mark A. (1994). *The Scandal of the Evangelical Mind*. Grand Rapids, MI: Eerdmans.

Pinnock, Clark (Ed). (1975). *Grace Unlimited*. Minneapolis, MN: Bethany Fellowship.

Schaeffer, Francis. (1972). *He is There and He is Not Silent*. Wheaton, IL: Tyndale House.

Sine, Tom. (1995). *Cease Fire: Searching for Sanity in America's Culture Wars*. Grand Rapids, MI: Eerdmans.

Stewart, Katherine. (2019). *The Power Worshippers: Inside the Dangerous Rise of Religious Nationalism.* New York, NY: Bloomsbury.

Sulloway, Frank J. (1997). *Born to Rebel: Birth Order, Family Dynamics, and Creative Lives.* New York, NY: Vintage.

Warren, Rick. (2002). *The Purpose Driven Life.* Grand Rapids, MI: Zondervan.

Willimon, Will. (2019). *Accidental Preacher: A Memoir.* Grand Rapids, MI: Eerdmans.

Wright, Lawrence. (1993). *Saints and Sinners.* New York, NY: Vintage.

Zahnd, Brian. (2016). *Water to Wine: Some of My Story.* St. Joseph, MO: Spello Press.

Doctoral Dissertation:

Peters, Daniel Barth. (1996). *Danny Orlis, The Yielded Woodsman: The Fundamentalist Self in Opposition to American Culture.* (Unpublished doctoral dissertation). Claremont Graduate School, Claremont, CA.

Music recordings:

Bachman-Turner Overdrive. (1973). *Gimme Your Money Please.* On *Bachman-Turner Overdrive* [CD]. Mercury Records.

Bachman-Turner Overdrive. (1975). *Lookin' Out for #1.* On *Head On* [CD]. Mercury Records.

Bachman-Turner Overdrive. (1973). *Takin' Care of Business.* On *Takin' Care of Business/Let it Ride* [CD]. Mercury Records.

Bachman-Turner Overdrive. (1974). *You Ain't Seen Nothing Yet.* On *Not Fragile* [CD]. Mercury Records.

Chapin, Harry. (1974). *Cat's in the Cradle.* On *Verities & Balderdash* [CD]. Elektra Records.

Holm, Dallas. (1986). *He'll Dry the Tears.* On *Against the Wind* [Record]. Dayspring/Word Records.

Joseph, Martyn. (2012). *Not a Good Time for God*. On *Songs for the Coming Home* [CD]. Pipe Records.

Reed, Lou. (1989). *Busload of Faith*. On *New York* [CD]. Sire–Warner Brothers Records.

Seger, Bob. (2017). *Busload of Faith*. On *I Knew You When* [CD]. Capital Records

Newspaper articles:

Meisnner, D. (2018, September 29). Where smartphones meet Sunday service. *The Globe and Mail*, p. A19.

Online magazine articles:

Heitler, Susan. (2018), February 01). Parental Alienation Syndrome: What Is It, and Who Does It?. Psychology Today. Retrieved from https://www.psychologytoday.com/us/blog/resolution-not-conflict/201802/parental-alienation-syndrome-what-is-it-and-who-does-it

Roys, Julie. (2019, January 31). Command and Control: Harvest Bible Chapel fires pastor at recently acquired church. WORLD Magazine. Retrieved from https://world.wng.org/2019/01/command_and_control

Roys, Julie. (2020, September 14). Betrayed Trust, Part One: New Testimony, Emails & Other Documents Portray Ravi Zacharias as Predator in Sexting Scandal. Retrieved from https://julieroys.com/ravi-zacharias-sexting-predator/ https://julieroys.com/ravi-zacharias-sexting-predator/

Roys, Julie. (2020, September 15). Betrayed Trust, Part Two: Woman Accused in Sexting Scandal Claims Ravi Zacharias Groomed & Exploited Her. Retrieved from https://julieroys.com/ravi-zacharias-groomed-woman/

Roys, Julie (2020, September 18). Betrayed Trust, Part Three: Ravi Zacharias Claimed Accusers in Sexting Scandal Were Extortionists, But Evidence Indicates Otherwise. Retrieve from https://julieroys.com/ravi-zacharias-extortionists-evidence-indicates-otherwise/

Shellnutt, Kate. & Eekhoff Zylstra, Sarah. (2017, December 03). Ravi Zacharias Responds to Sexting Allegations, Credentials Critique. Christianity Today. Retrieved from https://www.christianitytoday.com/news/2017/december/ravi-zacharias-sexting-extortion-lawsuit-doctorate-bio-rzim.html

Young, Valerie. (2015, June 10). What's A Mother Worth? Brain, Child. Retrieved from https://brainchildmag.com/ 2015/06/whats-a-mother-worth-2/

Online newspaper articles:

Brackear Pashman, Manya, & Coen, Jeff. (2018, March 23). After Years of Inquiries, Willow Creek Pastor Denies Misconduct Allegations. *Chicago Tribune*. Retrieved from http://www.chicagotribune.com/news/local/breaking/ct-met-willow-creek-pastor-20171220-story.html

Downen, Robert, & Olsen, Lise, & Tedesco, John. (2019, February 10). Abuse of Faith. *Houston Chronicle*. Retrieved from https://www.houstonchronicle.com/news/ investigations/ article/Southern-Baptist-sexual-abuse-spreads-as-leaders-13588038.php

Goodstein, Laurie. (2018, August 05). He's a Superstar Pastor. She Worked for Him and Says He Groped Her Repeatedly. *New York Times*. Retrieved from https://www.nytimes.com/ 2018/08/05/us/bill-hybels-willow-creek-pat-baranowski.html

Goodstein, Laurie, & Otterman, Sharon. (2018, August 14). Catholic Priests Abused 1,000 Children in Pennsylvania, Report Says. *New York Times*. Retrieved from https://www.nytimes.com/2018/08/14/us/catholic-church-sex-abuse-pennsylvania.html?searchResultPosition=2

McFarlan Miller, Emily. (2019, March 01). Misconduct Allegations Against Willow Creek Founder Bill Hybels Are Credible, Independent Report Finds. *The Washington Post*. Retrieved from https://www.washingtonpost.com/religion/2019/03/01/independent-report-finds-allegations-against-willow-creek-founder-bill-hybels-are-credible/

Oliver, Amy, & D'Antal, Stephen. (2017, August 19). The secret royal nephew: Zara's half-sister and lovechild of her father gives birth to a baby boy on the other side of the world (and his dad's a horseman too!). *The Daily Mail.* Retrieved from https://www.dailymail.co.uk/femail/article-4805746/Zara-Tindall-s-s-secret-little-nephew.html

Silets, Alexandra. (2018, August 13). More Resignations at Willow Creek Church in #MeToo Scandal. *WTTW News.* Retrieved from https://news.wttw.com/2018/08/13/more-resignations-willow-creek-church-metoo-scandal

Smith, Sarah. (2018, December 09). Hundreds of sex abuse allegations found in fundamental Baptist churches across U.S. *The Fort Worth Star-Telegram.* Retrieved from https://www.star-telegram.com/entertainment/living/religion/article222576310.html

Tom, Kai Cheng. (2018, October 26). The (trans) kids are all right: What gender-affirming health care really means. *The Globe and Mail.* Retrieved from https://www.theglobeandmail.com /opinion /article-the-trans-kids-are-all-right-what-gender-affirming-health-care/

Online news reports:

Roys, Julie. (2019, July 24). Willow Creek's Reconciliation Service Brings Closure to Some, But Alleged Victim Says "Hope Evaporated." Retrieved from http://julieroys.com/willow-creeks-reconciliation-service-brings-closure-to-some-but-alleged-victim-says-hope-evaporated/

Smietana, Bob. (2020, July 29). "Embattled Megachurch Pastor John Ortberg Resigns from Menlo Church. Retrieved from https://julieroys.com/embattled-megachurch-pastor-john-ortberg-resigns-from-menlo-church/

Online podcasts:

Roys, Julie. (2019, January 30). Listen to "The Church in Crisis" Online. [Audio podcast]. Retrieved from http://julieroys.com/ listen-church-crisis-online

For Further Reading

Christa Brown, *This Little Light: Beyond a Baptist Predator and His Gang* (Foremost Press, 2009).

Frederick Buechner, *A Crazy, Holy Grace* (Grand Rapids, MI: Zondervan, 2017).

Robert Farrar Capon, *Kingdom, Grace, Judgement: Paradox, Outrage and Vindication in the Parables of Jesus* (Grand Rapids, MI: Eerdmans, 2002).

Robert Farrar Capon, *The Parables of Grace* (Grand Rapids, MI: Eerdmans, 1991).

Kristal Chalmers with Eileen Peters, *Broken and Beautiful* (Victoria, Canada: Friesen Press, 2017).

Diane Darr Couts, *Things Fell Apart, But the Center Held* (Kindle Direct Publishing, 2020).

Rachel den Hollander, *What is a Girl Worth?* (Carol Stream, IL: Tyndale Momentum, 2019).

Ashley Easter, *The Courage Coach: A Practical, Friendly Guide on How to Heal From Abuse* (Scotts Valley, CA: CreateSpace, 2017).

Dale Ingraham and Rebecca Davis, *Tear Down This Wall of Silence: Dealing With Sexual Abuse in our Churches* (Greenville, SC: Ambassador International, 2015).

Diane Langberg, *Redeeming Power: Understanding Authority and Abuse in the Church* (Ada, MI: Brazos Press, 2020). (dianelangberg.com)

Max Lucado, *In the Grip of Grace: You can't fall beyond His love* (Dallas, TX: Word Publishing, 1996).

DeeAnn Miller, *How Little We Knew: Collusion and Confusion with Sexual Misconduct* (Prescott Press, 1993).

Wade Mullen, *Something's Not Right: Decoding the Hidden Tactics of Abuse* (Carol Stream, IL: Tyndale Momentum, 2020).

Clark H. Pinnock (ed.), *Grace Unlimited*. (Minneapolis, MN: Bethany Fellowship Inc., 1975).

Richard Rohr, *Radical Grace: Daily Meditations* (Cincinnati, OH: St. Anthony Messenger Press, 1995).

Lee Stroebel, *The Case for Grace: A Journalist Explores the Evidence of Transformed Lives* (Grand Rapids, MI: Zondervan, 2015).

Charles Swindoll, *The Grace Awakening* (Nashville, TN: W Publishing Group, 1996).

Beverly Shellrude Thompson, *Fly Away, Little Bird* (Victoria, Canada: Friesen Press, 2020).

Philip Yancey, *Vanishing Grace: Bringing Good News to a Deeply Divided World* (Grand Rapids, MI: Zondervan, 2018).

Philip Yancey, *What's So Amazing About Grace* (Grand Rapids, MI: Zondervan, 1997).

All God's Children (DVD) allgodschildrenthefilm.com

GRACE (Godly Response to Abuse in the Christian Environment) netgrace.org

Jimmy Hinton (pastor) jimmyhinton.org

Peter Janci (attorney, Oregon) crewjanci.com

Dee Parsons (blogger) thewartburgwatch.com

Missionary Kids Safety Net mksafetynet.org

Julie Roys (journalist) julieroys.com

Neil Schori (pastor) NeilSchori.com

Boz Tchividjian (attorney, Florida) landispa.com

Lori Anne Thompson (survivor & abuse researcher) loriannethompson.com

Index

A

abortion, 33
Abraham
    a spiritual loser, 73
    aborted of Isaac, 108
    moral ambiguity, 62, 71–73
    Romans 4, 47
    self-serving manipulator, 61
abstinence, 128
Academy Awards, 30, 151, 162
Alter, Robert, 69
American exceptionalism, 103
American Medical Association, 162
American Religious Right, 85
Anderson, David Robert, 65
Anne, Princess, 166
Aquinas, Thomas, 51
Armstrong, Karen, 17, 56, 60, 78
Aylward, Gladys, 12

B

Baby Gap, 156
Bachman-Turner Overdrive, 61, 68, 134, 144
Bakker, Jim and Tammy, 72
Bali, 94
Balmer, Randall, 33
Baptist Churches, independent fundamentalist, 31
Barnhouse, Donald Grey, 106
Baton Rouge, 94
Baughman, Steve, 31
Beatles, The, 156
Beauty Queen of Canaan, 60
behavioural legacy, 109
believers
    Am I loser friendly?, 99
    attitudes towards gays, 101
    gross immorality among God's people, 163
    self-righteous, 101
    zealous, 101
best-sellers
    It's All About You!, 61
Biblical icons, 53
Black Death, 64
Bly, Robert, 86
Bonhoeffer, Dietrich, 43, 176
    costly grace, 43
book series
    Chip Hilton, 13
    Danny Orlis, 13
    Felicia Cartwright, 13
    Hardy Boys, 13
    Sugar Creek Gang, 13
books
    Born to Rebel: Birth Order, Family Dynamics and Creative Lives, 124
    Genesis for Normal People: A Guide to the Most Controversial, Misunderstood, and Abused Book of the Bible, 22
    Genesis: A Living Conversation, 18
    God is Not a Vending Machine, 91
    I Was Wrong, 72
    Purpose Driven Life, The, 3
    Redeeming Power: Understanding Authority and Abuse in the Church, 162
    Sibling Society, The, 86
Borden of Yale, 13
Branch Davidians, 93
bubonic plague, 64
Buechner, Frederick, 34, 38, 113, 134, 135
Bullock, Sandra, 156
Byas, Jared, 22, 23, 25, 68, 81, 108, 138, 143, 147, 158

C

Callaway, Phil, 11, 159
Callaway, Tim

God is Loser Friendly

absence of disclaimer, 4
author, 11
commentator-journalist, 105
interpretive perspectives on
   Genesis, 45–52
pastor, 105
Calvinistic, 43
Canadian Army, 75
capitalist society, 6
Carmichael, Amy, 13
Catholics, 30
Chapin, Harry, 109
Chapin, Sandy, 109
chattel, 78
Chicago Tribune, 161
child psychologists, 108
child welfare, 107
Christianity, 55
Columbia University, 117
Columbine, 94
concentration camps, 93
   Auschwitz, 93
   Ravensbrück, 93
culture wars, 103

D

definitions
   "amusing" grace, 40
   busload of grace, 34
   disgrace, Genesis is unsanitized, 75
   disgrace, the Church by leaders, 32, 64
   grace is received not won, 39
   grace, author's definition, 40, 44
   grace, available when we bungle things, 89
   grace, busload of grace, 54
   loser, 5, 19, 43, 44, 53
   shyster, 18, 53, 142, 150
   worm theology, 5, 43
Department of Vital Statistics, 118
Deus Absconditus, 51
Discipline Review Committee, 170
disgrace, apply lipstick to a pig, 32
Dishonour Roll, 20
doubt, 65
Dr. Phil, 154

E

Ecclesiastes, 100
El Paso, 94
Elliot, Elisabeth, 179
Elliot, Jim and Elizabeth, 13
emojis and emoticons
   eye-roll, 3, 53
   smack-my-forehead, 53
Encarta dictionary, 18
Enns, Peter, 22, 23, 25, 68, 81, 108, 138, 143, 147, 158
Ezekiel 16:48f, 102

F

faith, the futility of, 79
Falwell, Jerry, Jr., 32
Family Counseling, 161
family reunions, 151
family values, 56
fear, 65, 112
Feiler, Bruce, 80
Focus on the Family, 61, 86
Fort Worth Star-Telegram, 31
Fortune magazine, 68
fundagelical, 11, 53, 177, 181

G

Gardner, Dr. Richard, 117
Garner, Jennifer, 156
Genesis
   emergence of grace, 35–37
   shortcomings of ancients, 5
Germo, Pastor Jeff, 21
God
   behaviour is perplexing, 141
   extends grace lavishly, 139
   grace is dumbfounding, 149
   hiddenness of God, 51
   is inexplicably gracious, 135
   Is silence not consent?, 140
   more longsuffering than us, 102
   silence on wrongdoing, 48, 95
   stubbornly loser friendly, 96
   unfairly dealing with humans, 69
   using jackasses a long time, 160
Golden Foot in Mouth Award, 120
Good Morning, Haran, 60
Google, 153, 168

Index

grace, 27
    always obtainable for losers, 68
    counter-intuitive to our experience, 41, 42
    extending grace is not easy, 181
    forgiveness and restoration, 68
    Genesis, 36
    Revelation, 36
Graham, Franklin, 32
Great Tribulation, The, 14
Griffith-Thomas, W.H., 39
Grounds, Vernon C., 39
Guyana, 93

H

Hamilton, Victor P., 38, 56, 61
Handicap Only parking spot, 148
Harrelson, Woody, 58
Harvest Bible Chapel, 32
Hebrews 11, 55
Henpecked Husbands Anonymous, 152
Hestenes, Roberta, 141
Hinten, Marvin, 91
Hiroshima, 93
Hollywood, 44, 58, 138
Holm, Dallas, 174
homosexuality, 33, 128
    condemning rhetoric, 98
Honour Roll, 19
    of Losers, 20
    of Winners, 20
Houston Chronicle, 32
human sexuality, 102, 128
Hybels, Bill, 29

I

imago Dei, 5
In Gold We Trust, 121
inequities of life, 85
infertility, 87, 88, 158
iPhone, 7
Islam, 55
It's not about you!, 3, 26, 119

J

Jacob
    a.k.a. Jake, the Snake, 133
    free pass from God, 149
    no sense of ethics or decency, 149
    ripping people off, 146, 147
Jake the Snake, 133, 136, 148
Jeffress, Robert, 32
JEPD, 20
Job's wife, 85
Jones, Jim, 93
Jonestown, 93
Joseph (Rachel's son), 159
Joseph, Martyn, 34
Judah
    association with Jesus Christ, 170
    dirty old man, 167
Judaism, 55
Judeo-Christian ethics, 52
Julian of Norwich, 64, 65
just say 'no', 128

K

Kaiser, Walter C., Jr., 51, 59, 70, 100
Kass, Leon R., 127
Klein, Naomi, 7
Koresh, David, 93
Kselman, John S., 16
Kuhn, Isobel, 13

L

L'Oréal, 156
Lac Magantic, Quebec, 94
Lamott, Anne, 11, 55, 75, 93, 107, 117, 133, 151, 161, 175
Langberg, Dianne (psychologist), 162
Livingstone, David, 12
London, 94
losers, we all can be, 75, 76
Lower Manhattan, 94

M

MacDonald, Pastor James, 32
Machiavelli, 127
Machiavellian ethic, 33
Maclean's, 19
Madison Avenue, 156
manifest destiny, 103
Matthew, 49
McMahon, Vince, 133
Mikolaski, Sam, 37
modern cosmetics industry, 156

monotheistic religions, 55
Moore, Demi, 58
Moral Majority, The, 103
Most Wanted List, 149
movies
   Fifty Shades of Grey, 151
   Indecent Proposal, 58
   Rambo, 138
   Spotlight, 30, 162
   Terminator, 138
Moyers, Bill, 18, 19, 76, 140
Mukjerkee, Bharati, 76
music
   All You Need Is Love, 156
   Amazing Grace, 43, 171
   At the Cross, 43
   Cat's in the Cradle, 109
   Dare to Be a Daniel, 14
   Gimme Your Money Please, 144
   He'll Dry the Tears, 173
   How Did Moses Cross the Red Sea?, 14
   I Knew You When, 34
   I Will Make You Fishers of Men, 14
   It's Not a Good Time for God, 34
   Lookin' Out for #1, 61, 67
   Only a Boy Named David, 14
   Rock of Ages, 42
   Takin' Care of Business, 68
   You ain't seen nothin' yet!, 134

N

Nagasaki, 93
Nairobi, 94
naming children, 118, 160
National Enquirer, 76
Neighbourhood Watch, 136
Netflix, 45, 118
New York Times, 30
Newton, John, 43
Nice, 94
Nintendo, 123
Noll, Mark, 32

O

Obama presidency, 33
Orlando, 94
Ortberg, John, 32
Osteen, Joel, 155

P

Parental Alienation Syndrome (PAS), 117
Parental Alienation Syndrome Association, 117
parental hypocrisy, 129, 131
Paris, 94
Pearl Harbour, 93
Peoples Temple, The, 93
Pharaoh, consequences of Abraham's wrongdoing, 77
Phillips, Mark (Captain), 166
Pittsburgh, 94
PMS (pre-menstrual syndrome), 153
politicization of religion, 104, 105
Post Traumatic Stress Disorder, 108
Promise Keepers, 56
PTL television empire, 72
Public Broadcasting System, 18
publishers, Christian
   Moody Press, 13
   Zondervan, 13

R

Rauser, Randal, 31
Ravi Zacharias International Ministries, 30
reckless grace, 175
Redford, Robert, 58
Reed, Lou, 29, 34
Relationship Enrichment Seminar, 157
religious elite, 101
religitics, 33, 103
Revelation, 100
Revlon, 156
Rivers III, Eugene, 62, 73
Roman Catholic Church, 15, 30
Roman Catholics, 181
Romans, 55
Rosenblatt, Naomi H., 127
Ruiz, Jean-Pierre M., 145

S

Sandy Hook, 94
Sarah's meltdown, 81
Schaeffer, Francis, 50
Seger, Bob, 34
Seitzinger, Tina, 123

self-preservation, 66
sexual abuse, 161, 163
    Roman Catholic clergy, 161
sexual assault, 162
sibling rivalry, 124
Simpson, Homer, 6, 27
Sine, Tom, 104, 130
Smedes, Lewis, 57, 73
Soap Opera Digest, 151
Sodom and Gomorrah, 94
Sony PlayStation, 123
Southern Baptist Convention, 32, 162
Springer, Jerry, 76
Steele, Danielle, 151
Stewart, Katherine, 33
Sulloway, Frank J., 124
Swaggart, Jimmy, 165

T

Taylor, J. Hudson, 12
television
    Big Love, 152
    Greenleaf, 118
    Lone Ranger, 138
    Sister Wives, 152
The Great Commission, 32
Thompson, Marianne Meye, 126
TMZ.com, 76, 135
Torn Between Four Lovers, 151
trans-gender, 128
Trump, Donald, 32

V

Visotzky, Burton L., 79, 140

W

Waco, Texas, 93
Wall Street, 58
Warren, Rick, 3, 6, 26, 40, 176
Watts, Isaac, 43
Willimon, Will, 34, 149
Willow Creek Church, 29
Winfrey, Oprah, 118
women's HELP-line, 77
World War II, 75, 93
World Wrestling Entertainment
    (WWE), 124, 133
World Wrestling Federation (WWF),
    133

Y

Yancey, Philip, 40, 177
Young, Valerie, 121
YouTube, 109

Z

Zacchaeus, 101
Zacharias, Ravi, 30
Zahnd, Brian, 9, 36

Made in the USA
Monee, IL
12 November 2020